"It's about time this book was written! Finally, someone is telling the true story of what it's really like to be an entrepreneur. I am super proud to have Kate Toon as our spokesperson. Kate tells it how it is (wobbly bits and all), making this book super relatable, highly captivating and downright amusing."

Loren Bartley | impactiv8.com.au businessaddicts.com

"If you've ever felt that you don't tick all (or any) of the 'proper entrepreneur' boxes then this funny, human and reassuring book will make you feel better about yourself. Much better. It's like having a chat with a supportive, wise and startlingly honest friend who's been there, done that and now runs three successful businesses. A refreshingly candid gem."

Dawn Kofie | www.zestywriting.com

"*Confessions of a Misfit Entrepreneur* is a funny, honest, easy-to-read account of what it's really like to be an entrepreneur. It's a must read for everyone starting their own business, and everyone who feels like they don't fit the traditional mould of what an entrepreneur should do, how they should look and how they should run their business.

Melinda Samson | Click-Winning Content

"*Confessions of a Misfit Entrepreneur* is amazeballs, and relatable on way too many levels!

If like me, you are tired of seeing only the highlight show reels of successful entrepreneurs, especially when some of those show reels and successes are pure fiction, then this is the book for you. It has all the feelings, the good, the bad, the ugly and the laugh out louds. (I have to admit to snort laughing on more than one occasion.)

Not only is this a great read, it also has helpful "over to you" worksheets incorporated throughout, which I loved."

Kerry Pietrobon | Harlowstore.com

"Who would have thought a book about boob envy and eyebrows down your back could be so refreshingly blatant about the truth or dare game we play when building and growing a business.

As I read each page I started to realise that all the blueprints, formulas and 'must dos' are just a pile of piglet poo. Sure it can be useful to grow your roses, but the stink and upset tummy along the way probably isn't really worth it.

I now wear my Misfit badge of honour with pride as I delete the 10,000 emails wanting to sell me something and go about my merry way building what I want to build, in a way that works for me."

Natasha Vanzetti | www.natashavanzetti.com

"I love how you completely open up and show your 'behind the scenes thoughts' (if that's even a thing). I love how refreshingly honest you are, funny and quirky, while offering genuinely valuable advice and inspiration.

Any entrepreneur should read this book. Anyone who wants to be one should read this book. And everyone else too. Bravo!"

Eva Schafroth | www.evaschafroth.com

"The first thought that leapt into my head when I started reading *Confessions of a Misfit Entrepreneur,* was 'Hoorah! I'm not a-f*cking-LONE!'"

I get a lot of people approaching me for help who have been hoodwinked by the kind of 'five-minute-work-week-sipping-pina-coladas-on-a-beach-in-Thailand-because-I-have-an-e-Course' hype that is promulgated by supermodel-esque business coaches in glossy Fakebook ads.

So much talking and truth telling is necessary, I may just have to make this book prerequisite reading material.

Never have I giggle-snorted my way through a book before. It's a soothing elixir for the weary businessperson's mind, and a staunch preventative for the wanna-be anythingpreneur or anyone thinking about becoming a small business owner.

It's chapter after chapter of reality checks that lift the veil on the truth behind running a small business. Lines like these, on getting a negative review: '...but I'm 100% cool with that because I'm running a business, not a popularity contest...', just made we want to reach through the screen and plant a whopping great sloppy one on your (face) cheek Kate. Love the style, the honesty, the pure dry wit of every chapter.

Bold, honest, and hands down the best business advice book I've read... well, ever."

Maria Doyle | mariadoyle.com

"*Confessions of a Misfit Entrepreneur* is fantastic. It's a relatable read – very funny at times, and offers great advice to people just starting out, or established in business.

Kate's experiences will help readers allay the feelings of self-doubt, demystifying the entrepreneurial jargon that is currently floating around.

I've just taken the jump from a full time day job with a side hustle to working a part time day job with a main hustle, and this book is a great resource to boost my confidence and reassure me I only need a (sales) funnel from the kitchen gadget store."

Carly Findlay | www.carlyfindlay.com.au

"A massively reassuring read if you run your own business and ever question whether you're doing it 'properly'. It's also funny, inspiring and very readable. Kate Toon's debunking of the many myths of entrepreneurial success manages to hide lots of really useful business advice in a very entertaining read. It's also fantastically irreverent."

Lucy Davies | www.websitesbylucy.co.uk

"Finally, someone who gets it. It's reassuring that I'm not the only crazy who thinks business can be done this way. *Confessions of a Misfit Entrepreneur* is the sanity check all entrepreneurs need. Kate Toon makes you feel totally understood and a little bit of a bad ass for wanting to go against the curve. While she hasn't quite converted me to her love of crisps, she has left me with a sense of knowing that doing my own awkward thing I'll be ok!"

Yael Keon | www.mixsavvymarketing.com

"I read this book in a single sitting and ignored my kids' pleas for sustenance. Kate's witty, clever and down to earth advice is a fresh anecdote to all the slick, salesy promises of other entrepreneurial tomes. Kate went from business zero to hero by avoiding the typical 'business rules' and following her instincts.

This is a must read for any wannabe entrepreneur who needs good solid advice mixed in with plenty of real life stories and lol-worthy giggles.

My favourite bits were the glossary at the end, the practical advice for getting stuff done, and of course the hilarious Toonisms and footnotes littered throughout."

Kate Merryweather | www.dotcomwords.com.au

"You speak our language as we see our lives day in day out! The juggle, the hustle, the 'I am NOT going back to corporate" (but I can't put food on the table this week – that might be a bit of an issue)!!

Being on this journey is bloody hard and the words/style/comments you have used will resonate with so many of us doing our 'thang'!"

Dani Tamati | www.therh.com.au

"With my editing hat on, Kate Toon delights me. Her voice is distinctive, her words considered, and she knows exactly how to connect with an audience. With my writing hat on, Kate makes me despair for the exact same reasons. I continually find myself resisting the urge to 'write like Kate Toon' because, as we all know, there can only ever be one of those! *Confessions of a Misfit Entrepreneur* is Kate at her hilarious and practical best."

Kelly Exeter | www.flyingsolo.com.au

"You're not the only one feeling fed up with all the hyped up smoke and mirrors, entrepreneurial 'advice'.

Kate Toon felt like this too and has put fingers to keyboard to challenge the myths surrounding entrepreneurs. She walks her talk and with refreshing honesty reveals the highs, lows, sideway steps and reality of what it's like to really run your own business.

With humour, kindness and down to earth strategies Kate shows you how you can run a business on your own terms."

Kylie Saunder | www.kyliesaunder.com

"This book is ESSENTIAL reading for entrepreneurs. Particularly those who have over-invested, under-achieved and beaten themselves up for not having the social media lifestyle that so many of the marketers we follow 'appear' to have. Every chapter of Kate's book is a new permission slip I didn't even know I needed. Without an iota of blaming, whining or self-flagellation, Confessions is the online business story we all need to know. Oh, and you'll roll about on the floor laughing while reading too!"

Katie Wyatt | www.katiewyatt.me

CONFESSIONS OF A MISFIT ENTREPRENEUR

HOW TO SUCCEED IN BUSINESS DESPITE YOURSELF

KATE TOON

National Library of Australia

Cataloguing-in-Publication entry information

has been applied for

ISBN: 978-0-6480261-0-5 (paperback)

Printed in Australia

First Edition

Cover Design: Kate Buckland

Cover photo: Sherbet Birdie

Book Design & Layout: Swish Design

To Pamplemousse, my furry business partner, mentor, life coach and CFO (Chief Furry Officer).

ABOUT THE AUTHOR

Kate Toon is an award-winning SEO copywriter and SEO consultant with almost two decades of experience in all things advertising, digital and writing.

Originally from the UK, but now based just outside Sydney, Kate has worked with big brands such as eHarmony, Curash and Kmart. And she's helped countless small businesses produce great content and improve their copywriting and SEO.

Kate is also the founder of *The Clever Copywriting School* and *The Recipe for SEO Success eCourse,* as well as co-host on the *Hot Copy Podcast.*

She presents the *Write for Business* show for Dale Beaumont's B.ai app, and recently launched The Copywriting Conference – Australia's first dedicated copywriting conference.

Find out more about Kate at www.katetoon.com.

FACEBOOK GROUP

Want to join the Misfit movement? Join my FB group at facebook.com/groups/confessionsofamisfitentrepreneur

DONATIONS

$1 from every book purchased will be donated to Rafiki Mwema, a charity that was born from the need to support very young girls and boys in Kenya who have suffered huge trauma.

Rafiki Mwema means 'Loyal Friend' (in Swahili) and that is what we are to these young girls and boys.

All our children live as one 'Rafiki family', but in separate houses. They are therapeutically parented and receive regular therapy as individuals and in groups. They are supported to have safe contact with their families. Above all they are loved.

We work with their families, the communities, schools, churches, villages, and government officials with the aim to break this cycle of abuse and let children live as children should.

We are totally committed to supporting children who have experienced things we could not even imagine, to help heal their trauma and allow them to grow to love and be loved.

www.rafikimwema.com

CONTENTS

FOREWORD

Every couple of years for the past decade, we've researched our Flying Solo community of entrepreneurs and soloists and asked them what appeals most about running their own business. Why did they start, or what attracts them to the idea of starting their own show.

Firmly at the top of their responses and in an order that has yet to change, are 'freedom', 'flexibility' and 'control'.

And it's no wonder. Why wouldn't you opt to do work you enjoy, alongside people you like, from the location of your choice? Working the hours you choose, charging the fees you want and showing up wearing whatever takes your fancy.

Pursuing and creating a vocation that looks like this, is surely living the dream?

In his New York Times bestseller, *Drive: The Surprising truth about what motivates us* Dan Pink distils and comments on the findings of numerous behavioural science and psychology studies and concludes that what inspires and motivates us humans is a sense of autonomy, mastery and purpose.

In other words what makes us truly happy and productive bunnies, is having control over what we do, using and improving our skills and doing work that has meaning.

There's that dream again.

Add to that the desire and realisation of some decent revenue generation and surely there's your professional nirvana right there.

And how hard can it be? After all everyone's doing it. Small, entrepreneurial enterprises – mostly solo, one person ventures – dominate the small business landscape across the world and the stampede gains more momentum each and every day.

In Australia, over 70% of small businesses fit into this category and those are just the ones who show up in statistics. Conservatively, we're talking about over 2 million people. That's a lot of people in a country with not a lot of people.

In the United States, estimates put their figure at over 50 million individuals choosing to work independently. No job. No boss. No worry.

But really are all these entrepreneurs, soloists, freelancers, side-hustlers, indie professionals, contingent workers, creative and free agents[1] really living the dream? Are they all cruising around in a state of perpetual bliss, smashing goals and making a motza? Er, well no. Not all of them. Not by a long shot.

Running your own show isn't a walk in the park. It takes planning, effort, commitment and resilience and at the core of success is understanding that this really is Your. Own. Show. This stuff is personal.

What works for someone else, may not work for you.

In the pages that follow, my good friend and fellow solo traveller, Kate Toon shares her very unique take on the world of work. Whether you recognise yourself as similarly misfitting, massively more misfitting or merely detouring slightly from the norm (whatever that is), I promise you you're going to feel mollified, energised and entertained as a consequence of this book.

Trawl bookshops and libraries the world over and you'll not find a business book that's as candid, irreverent and downright useful as

---

[1] Pick your nomenclature of choice, the list is endless

Confessions of a Misfit Entrepreneur.

In her Introduction, Kate wonders 'if you could actually be an entrepreneur if you don't really feel like one'.

Well, clearly you can, because she's one of the best I know.

Enjoy your journey.

Robert Gerrish

Founder, Flying Solo: Australia's solo and micro business community (www.flyingsolo.com.au).
Author & presenter of *Work your way: The complete guide to going it alone in business* (www.soloism.com).

INTRODUCTION

Entrepreneurs are the rock stars of our time.

Wherever you look, you see them splashing about in all their entrepreneurial glory.

They take every opportunity to tell us:

- How they started with nothing and built an empire
- How they're living the four-hour working week dream
- How they succeeded in business by taking risks, dreaming big and reaching high

And it's all so confusing.

Because as I read these articles, dressed in my PJs and dropping biscuit crumbs onto my keyboard, I feel a twinge of envy.

But I also feel a quiver of revulsion.

Because I **should** want all of that, right?

My business dreams should be all about me. I'm on stage, my hair groomed to perfection and a lapel microphone dangling tantalisingly from my expensive smart casual wear, oozing confidence from every orifice.

And when I speak?

Naturally I'll shower the gobsmacked crowd with thigh-tinglingly inspiring little globs of Ted Talk[2] genius. And feel the utter adoration as they hurl cash in my general direction.

But then I wake up in a clammy sweat.

---

[2] Ted Talks are short presentations that involve Madonna headsets and lots of hand waving.

Because the truth is I don't want all of that.

In fact, this whole entrepreneur thing makes me feel a bit ill.

Okay, so let's take a minute. What actually is an entrepreneur?

Well, in dictionary terms it's simply "a person who sets up a business or businesses, taking on financial risks in the hope of profit".

So that's basically anyone who starts a business, right?

But these days it means so much more.

Entrepreneurs spend all day 'crushing it'.

And no, it doesn't matter what the 'it' is. When they're not making six figures from their hammocks they're posting 800-word Facebook ads telling you how you can do it too.

These days everyone is an entrepreneur. (Unless of course they're a coach.) My mum is an entrepreneur, as is my hairdresser's cousin, my vet and my dog. Even that piece of fluff I just sucked up with the vacuum cleaner has a $10,000 mastermind plan.

And if they're not an entrepreneur they're a solopreneur, or maybe a mumpreneur.

Take any word and place it before 'preneur', and you can be one too.

Dancepreneur: "I have a YouTube channel where I dance around in my pants in the kitchen. Buy my eight-week course."

Cakepreneur: "I make cakes shaped like internal organs. Download my cheat sheet."

Gitpreneur: "I'm not a very nice person. Join my webinar to find out how you too can be nasty and earn $10k a nanosecond."

But the truth is that the notion of entrepreneurialism (a word I still struggle to say out loud) never crossed my mind. And becoming an entrepreneur was never part of my game plan.

Psst: Even now, whenever I type 'entrepreneur' I make little air quotes in my mind.

You see, when I started my business I had one simple goal – survival.

I just wanted to leave behind the horrors of the boardroom, and make enough money to live comfortably.

To be honest, I never even *had* a game plan.

As for the personal attributes of the entrepreneur... well, I'm not particularly glamorous, confident or wise. My spirit of adventure rarely extends beyond taking my dog Pamplemousse on a new route for his daily walk.

And the thought of taking a risk actually makes my nipples invert.

I've stumbled, bumbled and fumbled my way through running a business. There have been moments of both utter joy and terrible crushing misery. I think I've experienced every emotion possible, and discovered a few new ones I never knew existed.

Oh, and I've done it all without a business coach (unless you count my dog, who's a great listener but occasionally wees on my printer).

There's never been anyone to guide me through the choppy business seas to the calm pond of success. I've paddled my own business canoe all the way. And quite frankly my arms are tired.

But I've made it work.

Without wanting to toot my own horn, I've developed not one but three successful businesses.

I've built a reputation in my (relatively small) circles for doing what I do well.

I've created courses, shops and membership programs. I have podcasts and passive income, and regularly speak at events.

And, without wanting to sound boastful, I consistently earn the mythical six figures. (Profit, not revenue.)

Now, I don't measure financial security in private jet miles. For me it's all about not having to check the receipt at Coles[3], and being able to enjoy a wine-fuelled online shopping spree without crippling the family finances.

But I am making way more money than I ever did as an ad agency manager – all in my crumb-covered PJs from a hut in my back garden.

While I haven't quite cracked the four-hour work week, I am working just a few short days a week bookended by school pick-ups and drop-offs. There's no commute, no working on weekends, and no burning the midnight oil. These days I'm in bed by 8pm watching *Suits* on Netflix.

Most importantly, my business success lets me work how I want, when I want. No greasy boss man (or woman) to set my objectives, and no-one to answer to except me, myself and I.

I have the money, the freedom, the lifestyle and occasionally the warm glow of success from doing it all on my lonesome.

So that **kind** of makes me an entrepreneur, doesn't it?

I'm still not 100% sure.

Because I'm the first to admit that a lot of it happened by happy accident rather than design. I've never followed the so-called rules of business. Most of the time I've either ignored them or deliberately broken them.

And today, eight years into my solo business journey, I still seem to snark at the sensible business advice given by the gurus.

I look at the well-known entrepreneur types and see nothing of myself in them. If they're the cool kids in high school, I'm the weirdo sitting on my own in the cafeteria making bracelets out of drinking straws.

---

[3] For my overseas buddies, Coles is an Australian supermarket.

I've read the entrepreneurial checklists and can barely tick a box.

So, I began to wonder if you could actually be an entrepreneur if you don't really feel like one.

And that's why I'm writing this book.

As small business owners, there's so much pressure on us to be the next big thing – to reach higher and push harder. We're made to believe we can all have a piece of the entrepreneurial pie as long as we sign up to some webinar and pay a fortune to learn from some guru with aggressively white teeth.

I ain't buying it. Literally and figuratively.

I don't believe you need to pay for the mastermind class, play by the rules, or follow the so-called leader.

I believe there are many different ways to the top, and that your top doesn't need to be the same as everyone else's.

I'm sharing my story so I can pass on what I've learned along the way, and give you some little tips and prods that may make your business life easy. By sharing my business highs and woes, I hope I can offer you a little reassurance, or at the very least make you feel a little less shitty about your own business journey.

Most of all, I hope I can make you smile, and maybe even snort tea onto your own crumb-covered keyboard. Because let's face it: running a business can be stressful, boring and difficult (a nice way of saying that sometimes it totally sucks balls). And being able to laugh and take the piss out of both myself and my business has always helped me get through the tough times.

HOW THIS BOOK WORKS

In each chapter I'll take one of the traits ascribed to entrepreneurs, the 'requirements', and then poke it and pull it apart to see how relevant or necessary it really is.

You won't find any get-rich-quick schemes in this book. I won't be selling you some impossible dream of working ten minutes a day from a hammock either.

And if you're looking for a serious, hard-hitting business tome or philosophical deep-dive you should head back to Amazon. This book is business light – and proud to be.

WHO SHOULD READ THIS BOOK?

If you've ever looked at those 'Top 10 Entrepreneurs' lists and struggled to identify with any of them, then this book is for you.

It's for people trying to juggle shopping, getting the dog shampooed and fixing broken washing machines with building lead generation pages, scheduling social media and updating plugins.

It's for people who get a tight feeling in their tummy when they scroll through Facebook late at night and see their competitors rising up the ranks.

And it's for people who struggle to make sense of their place in the business world, question what's normal, and keep asking themselves, "Am I good enough?"

In other words, it's for normal human beings like you and me.

This book is for those of us who don't fit the standard entrepreneur mould. Who want to be reassured they can still be a success without being a jet-setting entrepreneur with a membership program, a master class, and a warehouse full of trendy youths squatting on bean bags in the up-and-coming part of town.

And by the end of the book you'll know you *can* be a success – on your own terms.

P.S. Yes, you *are* good enough.

SIDE NOTE: SOUR GRAPES

Okay, let's address the elephant in the room. Some of you may be thinking, "She's just bagging out the whole entrepreneur dream because she hasn't made it big herself".

Perhaps you think this book is driven by bitterness, envy, and a modicum of jealousy.

So, **do** I have a bad case of sour grapes?

Well, yes. Maybe. Or at least I did.

For a long time I suffered from severe entrepreneurial envy.

As I attended more and more business events, I found myself rubbing shoulders (and **only** shoulders) with horribly successful people.

I went from following these people from afar on social media to mingling, having dinner and suffering late night karaoke sessions with them.

I went from being a small fish in a giant pond to being a small fish in an expensive mineral-water-filled lake full of confident coy carp.

And it messed with my tiny fishy mind.

At first I coped just fine with these situations.

I focused on spooning soup noiselessly into my mouth while those around me talked about their eight trillion Facebook followers.

I nodded politely when they regaled me with tales of making

$68,000 in membership revenue in the time it took me to butter my bread roll.

I smiled. I made appreciative noises.

But inside I was nonplussed. They were them. I was me. Yes, I was smaller. But business isn't a competition, right?

Right?

Unfortunately, it wasn't long before I started to think, "Wrong".

Having been exposed to this excessive entrepreneurial talk for so long, it began to seep into my inner being through the cracks in my confidence.

Surrounded by people obsessed with big numbers, retention, automation and building a business empire, my own business cul-de-sac just didn't seem enough.

I wanted what they had.

I wanted to be a **real** entrepreneur.

They say that when people are far away from you, you admire them. But the closer they get, the more you envy them.

Well, I can admire Beyonce's talent because I have no desire to be a singer. But when I see someone a few rungs up the marketing-type-person ladder, it feels doable.

The symptoms of my entrepreneurial ailment began to present pretty quickly.

They included:

- Dry eyes from obsessively following social media
- Stomach pains from opening the emails of my entrepreneurial competitors
- Finger exhaustion from continually entering my credit card details to buy the latest CRM or automation software

- Carpal tunnel syndrome from trying to out-wit, out-write and out-awesome everyone
- Brain ache from performing endless pricing and ROI calculations
- Glazed eyes (other people's, not mine) from me talking endlessly about sales funnels, integration and click-through rates.

At first I considered treatment for my entrepreneur-envy condition, thinking that perhaps the only way to treat my entrepreneurial envy condition was to <shudders> become one of them.

A quick Google search gave me lots of options, all of which promised that if I followed their recommendations I too could join their hallowed clan and be cured.

Hallelujah! All praise Richard Branson!

I could:

- Attend 'free' business seminars on how to build my business empire
- Hand over $10,000 for flashy influencer programs sold by tanned men with slick hair and stubble that's just the right length
- Pay for business gurus who believe you're only successful if you earn seven figures (which you need to be earning to pay their absurdly high coaching cost)
- Join a Mastermind group of like-minded beasts in an attempt to suck success juice from my entrepreneur of choice.

I'm pretty sure some of these may have worked. But I'll never know because they all involved giving big chunks of cash to other people – something I don't particularly like doing.

And then, after a little belly button gazing, I realised I was already a success.

Even if I chose to dip my toe in the grimy pond of comparison, when I measured myself up against my peers I was doing okay.

And that measuring myself up against the likes of Richard Branson, Oprah and Gary Vaynerchuck was just plain stupid.

So, while I admit I've wasted large chunks of time envying the success of others, I've finally arrived at a place of acceptance. (How Oprah does that sound?)

I've learned to live my life, focus on my own race, and stop signing up to my competitors' newsletters just to make myself feel bad.

All the sour grapes have been removed from the bunch. And the grapes left behind are ripe, juicy, and ready for me to appreciate just how sweet they really are.

CHAPTER 1

THE ROCKY BOTTOM

ENTREPRENEURIAL REQUIREMENT

A rags-to-riches story

My bottom, though ample, is not rocky.

I wasn't raised by wolves. I didn't lose my home in a freak rhino stampede. I have all my limbs, and have never been particularly oppressed by anyone.

But that doesn't play well in entrepreneurial land.

To be a true entrepreneur you have to clamber out of the poo (like that kid in Slumdog Millionaire) and rise to the pinnacle of awesomeness.

You have to STRUGGLE before you SUCCEED.

It's all part of the entrepreneurial 'journey'.

Don't believe me? Start clicking on those long 'entrepreneur' ads on Facebook. They usually consist of a smooth-skinned, glossy-nosed entrepreneur[4] smiling winningly against a gradually fading background as you read the stock standard text that goes something like this:

> *"Back in <a date long enough ago to give gravitas, but recent enough to seem relevant> I was in a bad place.*

---

[4] Like overly keen puppies with glossy noses

I'd been fired from my job, dumped by my <girlfriend/boyfriend/ wife/husband>, crashed my <crappy car>, and my <fish/dog/ lemming> had died.

I only had $<ridiculous small figure> in the bank.

And that's when I <insert epiphany>.

Since then I've made $<suitably insane figure that isn't clear whether it's profit or revenue and isn't backed up by anything>.

And now I'm here to show you how you can make $<suitably insane figure> in <suitably ridiculous time frame> with my proven formula for <something>."

The other one goes like this. (This time I'll drop the brackets and just fill in the blanks:

"Back in 2006 I started my first business. My idea was selling hand-made hedgehog jumpers.

I didn't know how to knit, was allergic to wool, hated hedgehogs and had no fingers, but I wasn't going to let that stop me.

I did a search on Google for the dimensions of the average hedgehog and got started.

Everything looked awesome at first. I landed my first big order from a hedgehog farm in Botswana. I earned $30,000k in my first year!

But there was one big problem: I wasn't making a profit.

I was also working too hard, had no mates, and had developed a nasty rash on my inner thigh.

I was a lost puppy, and I knew things needed to change.

And that's when I realised that hedgehogs don't need jumpers – but piglets do.

Since then I've made $2,456,888.

And now I'm here to show you how you can make $67,884 in 24 hours with my proven formula for product launches."

I'm afraid I don't have a 'rock bottom' story.

I also don't have a series of failed businesses behind me.

When it comes to rags-to-riches stories, mine is... well, pretty average. No million-dollar losses or major epiphanies. Just a gentle plod through jobs and real life.

Boring, huh?

Well, yes and no. Because in my humble opinion not all stories need to be blockbusters, and often it's the teeny tiny lessons that teach us the most.

Admittedly, my clamber up the career mountain has been, if not rocky, then at least a touch gravelly.

I've had some truly terrible jobs, and wandered through the vocation wilderness for months at a time.

But each job was illuminating, and I don't think I'd be the business woman I am today without these often hideous experiences.

MY BROTHER – THE ORIGINAL ENTREPRENEUR

My first job was subcontracting for my brother. (Thanks, Chris.)

While he sat at home watching TV, I trudged around our neighbourhood posting the free paper in people's letterboxes. (And yes, I actually put it in their letterbox rather than just throw it on their lawn. I was a professional even then.)

These days a kid with a job like this would probably have their mum following in the family SUV to make sure they were safe. But back then, Mum was happy for me to wander the streets in the gloom of dusk while she cooked dinner and listened to Barry Manilow.

This was pre-iPod (and even pre-Walkman), so it was just me and the mean streets of my housing estate. The bag weighed as much as a small toddler, and I came home filthy from the newsprint.

But oh, how I loved that job.

My brother got paid two pounds a week – a princely sum at the time – of which he gave me 40p. (That's about two dollars in today's money.) Looking back it was a terrible deal, but I was just delighted to be earning extra money. That 40p could buy two Creme Eggs and a Jackie magazine, which was all I wanted out of life.

LESSON LEARNED: Subcontracting is the way go to. My brother was living the passive income dream back in 1985.

WHY I'M ALL TALK

After university I wanted to study journalism. But my morbid fear of debt meant I didn't dare take out a loan for the fees. So instead I drifted from office job to bar job to shop job.

I finally scored a semi-well-paying gig as a cloakroom girl where I could scam free drinks, read my book, and be rude to customers because the club was cool and they were not.

But I still needed extra cash, because back then 21-year-old me and Topshop were a dangerous combination.

My actress friend was working for an adult chat line at the time, and said it was a great opportunity for her to practice roleplay.

But for me, not so much.

I applied, was interviewed by a greasy faced man named Alan[5], and started at 3pm the following afternoon.

It was actually quite shocking to see how many blokes were feeling lustful at such an innocuous hour. And it was so, so, so incredibly unsexy. A room full of bored women eating pot noodles and cheese and onion crisps, some knitting, some doing crosswords while taking the call.

---

[5] Names have been altered to protect the innocent

And no, I wasn't lying on my back with my perfectly polished legs in the air, whispering sultry nothings into a retro phone. That vintage photo on the cover is a fat lie. I think someone physically had to hold my legs up and they've been photoshopped out. I was never a particular limber beast, even in my youth.

We were paid based on how long we could keep the punters talking, with bonuses if we made the magic hour-long mark.

My calls generally lasted around seven minutes.

While the bored middle-aged housewives around me purred sweet, filthy nothings into the moist, eager earholes of our customers, I awkwardly asked them about their holidays, whether they had brothers and sisters, and what their favourite flavour of jam was.

I couldn't connect with my audience, and simply didn't know how to talk dirty.

I was let go after my first shift.

LESSON LEARNED: It's vital to understand your audience, and be able to speak their language.

I LEFT UNI WITH NO IDEA WHAT I WANTED TO DO

I was 22 when I got my first job in 'advertising', working at the prestigious Saatchi and Saatchi in Soho's Golden Square. The office was fabulously schmick, and famous for its glass staircase where the ad execs would gather to look up the skirts of the female staff.

I was a PA to one of the Account Directors. His main account was promoting the Conservative party, and he was a cross between Boris Johnson and Don Draper.

In short, he was a pain in the bum cheek.

My role primarily involved:

- Going to Liberty to pick up his ties
- Fetching him sandwiches
- Lighting his cigarettes (I kid you not)

He took huge delight in pointing out my every mistake, and called me his 'silly little girl'. I regularly fantasised about pushing him down those glass stairs.

I escaped after three months into a publishing role and promised never to work in advertising again.

LESSON LEARNED: Don't work with dicks. (That sounds bad, but you know what I mean.)

MY FIRST REAL JOB

After a year or so in publishing the internet was invented, and I wanted a piece of the digital action.

I applied for a producer job at a super-trendy, up-and-coming internet agency, even though I had no clue what I was doing. And, by some crazy chance, I got the role.

My main project was to manage the Marks and Spencer website. I was immediately thrust into rooms of insanely clever designers, copywriters and programmers, where I was supposed to tell them all what to do.

In one of these early meetings I classically asked, "What's a browser?" The hushed silence that followed still haunts me to this day.

But my boss was awesome ("hey, Terry"), and saw potential in me.

He offered me a promotion after a few months, but I turned it down.

I'd blagged my way into the job, but the stress of those early months was horrendous.

Trying to pretend to be something you're not isn't fun. And trying to talk about something intelligently when you don't understand it yourself is hideous.

I really wanted to know what I was doing before I took the next step. So I waited, and several months later got the promotion that started my digital career.

LESSON LEARNED: While it's occasionally good to talk the talk before you can walk the walk, it's also good to know your limits.

THE ROCKY CAREER PATH

After this I headed to Australia as a backpacker, ran out of money within two weeks, and scored a role at Singleton Ogilvy.

Psst: At the time I had no idea why my boss took me on. I was scruffy, inexperienced and not particularly grown up.

But looking back I see that she was a bit of a misfit entrepreneur too. She worked in an all-male environment – I remember her being extremely wise and funny. If there's one business person I think of as a mentor (other than my dad) I'd say it was Sally Martyn – so thanks Sally.

It was a fairly high power job, and I knew I had to look the part. I asked Ma and Pa Toon for a loan to get myself a capsule work wardrobe[6], but they weren't forthcoming.

I was incredibly pissed off at the time, but now it makes a nice anecdote for my book.

I took what little money I had left to Portmans[7] to buy a cheap skirt and a couple of tops. But my budget didn't stretch far enough to buy shoes, and so I had to wear my battered Thailand flip-flops (or thongs here in Australia).

I'll never forget arriving (late) on my first day, heading through the

---

[6] A capsule work wardrobe is where you have eight items that all work together. I'm shocked you don't know what this is. Have you never read an inane women's fashion magazine?

wrong door at the Singleton Ogilvy bar, and walking right into John Singleton presenting to the entire staff. And yes I was wearing my shitty flip flops.

Sally, who was surely thinking "Who the hell have I employed?" then had to introduce me to the staff.

And having to wait three weeks for payday to come around meant I also developed an unsightly rash on my feet from wearing flip flops every day. It wasn't a great start to agency life and, if I'm honest, it never really got much better.

LESSON LEARNED: Don't wear flip-flops for prolonged periods, and even if you can't look 100% schmick for work at least be clean and tidy.

THE TURNING POINT

After that, it was an endless stream of agencies, one after another.

I won't say I didn't enjoy the endless beanbags and booze, at least not to begin with. I got to work on big name accounts in Australia, England and across Europe. And in doing so I worked with lots of amazingly clever humans, enjoyed some awesome experiences, and earned a great salary.

But it was a hard life and, quite frankly, a young person's game.

After ten years I found the environment soul sucking and stressful. I just didn't seem to be the right fit anymore. The bravado and the bullshit weren't my style. My skin wasn't thick enough. My wiggly bits weren't big enough.

I wasn't hot enough to be a sexy account manager, or cool enough to be a hip creative. I was just a scruffy, slightly frazzled producer with an increasingly bad temper.

---

[7] An Australian fashion store that sells affordable but possibly not great quality clothes

THE TWO TIMES I TRIED TO LEAVE

At one point I chucked everything in to become a masseuse. Unfortunately, having to oil up old, chubby people made it far less enjoyable than I thought it would be.

And then, after one particularly bad advertising role (think: board member, big salary, commission and a throng of ego-driven know-it-alls), I gave it all up to work in the warehouse of a large well-known florist's, packing roses into boxes during the Valentine's Day rush.

Suffice to say they treated their staff like slaves, and I worked harder in those two days than I have in all my years since.

But the hard-working women earning a pittance for their families were amazing. Most were immigrants, with only a few years in Australia under their belt. They were grateful to be in the country, and just as grateful for the work, their lives, their families and the opportunity.

Their immense and humble gratitude made me realise what an ungrateful moo I'd been, and that I was lucky to have such a cushy life.

LESSON LEARNED: How lucky I am to be living in a free country where women's rights are largely respected.

WORKING IN THE REAL WORLD

At 34ish, I was on my way to a General Manager role. I had a team of people working for me. I was earning a sackful of money, and working on high profile client accounts.

I should have been happy. But instead I found myself sobbing on the bus to work.

I was too scared to take the leap, and I kind of hated life.

DECEMBER 2005: UP THE DUFF

I distinctly remember going to a posh shop to buy some sucky-inny pants and feeling totally fed up.

Don't get me wrong. I've never been a washboard stomach kind of gal. But my pot belly was becoming decidedly plump, and no amount of exercise would get rid of it.

It turns out I was pregnant.

No great shakes you might think. But it was a big deal for my husband and me. I'd been told several years earlier that I couldn't have kids. To be honest I was utterly miserable about it, but I'd stuffed those feelings in an emotional sock and pushed it to the back of my emotional drawer.

And now, I was 'with child'.

I was working as a contractor, and living in a cramped but horribly expensive flat in Sydney. My husband ran his own business, but at the time it brought in less money than I now spend on crisps each week.

I was the breadwinner. So how was I going to make my dough?

POINTS TO PONDER

This is one of the most personal chapters in the book, and really focuses on my story.

Writing it was interesting and a bit daunting. So why don't **YOU** try it?

Take an hour or so to:

1. Write down each job you've had, starting from you first.
2. Remember one positive and one negative thing about the role.
3. List one lesson you learned from that role.

All too often we dismiss those crappy dishwashing jobs as a waste of time, and instead focus on the more grown-up jobs. But I've found it's been the broken rungs on my career ladder that have taught me the most.

WHAT THEY SAY 

To be a real entrepreneur you must start from nothing and work your way up. You must have a zero bank balance and take huge, thigh-shuddering risks to make it big.

WHAT I SAY 

Calculated risk isn't as sexy, but it's also a lot less stressful. It's fine to start small, keep your day job, and build things up before you take the plunge.

CHAPTER 2
PLAN? WHAT PLAN?

Can I let you in on a secret?

I've never had a business plan.

I've never taken the time to work out my goals. Instead I've lurched from one idea to the next, driven by instinct rather than intellect. I've tried a few times to get it all down on paper, but it's never happened.

I'm afraid the whole 'increase my email list by blah and reduce my bounce rate by x percent' stuff just bores me to tears.

But I did make one rather shameful attempt at a business mood board.

Rather than going digital, I went old school and used scissors, paper and glue. And I must say I found it hugely satisfying. I put it up on my office wall, and promptly ignored it for the rest of the year.

I don't believe you need a detailed business plan when you're getting started.

I think taking a more organic approach is A-OK. And by 'organic' I don't mean some kind of 'woo woo, hessian' approach. I mean going with the flow and trusting your business instincts.

If there's one thing I can say about my business journey it's that it hasn't been linear. I've gone the long way around a few times, but have also found some amazing shortcuts.

The business coaches will tell you it's vital to have a plan, or at the very least a vision. And that these are important business tools that will guide you through the tough times, and help you make clear decisions about what you should and shouldn't be doing.

Well, here's *my* vision: Work from home and make money.

It's not particularly edifying, is it? I'm not trying to save the world or build a legacy.

All I want, and all I've ever wanted, is a relatively happy and comfortable life.

So while I don't think you necessarily need a business plan, I do think you need a vision. Or as Simon Sinek puts it, a **'why'**. Or maybe even a list of 'why's.

These 'why's will help steer you in the early months, and bring you back to reality years from now.

My 'why's for doing what I do haven't changed much over the years. I do what I do so:

- I can spend time with my son
- I don't have to work for 'the man'
- I have the freedom to do my own thing, make my own decisions, and learn from my own mistakes
- I can earn a decent enough living to travel a bit, buy the odd thing, give a little away, and not have to worry

But let's get back to how I got started.

While pretending to work hard at my day job, I started to plan my escape.

A nice dude at work (thanks, Kane) built me a WordPress blog in a few minutes, and another nice dude (thanks, Roger) took a quick snap so I had a 'corporate headshot'.

I swiftly registered for an ABN online and BOOM! I was in business.

Here are some of the things I **didn't** do before I started my business:

- Work out my ideal customer avatar and map out my customer life cycle
- Spend thousands on a brand specialist to hone my brand
- Drop two grand on a course to 'up-level'
- Download every software package and app known to man, woman and beast
- Splash more cash on an expensive new laptop and sexy office equipment

I was five months pregnant with no savings, a relatively penniless husband, and no backup plan. So I just got started.

I didn't have the luxury of time, or a soft cushion of money to fall back on.

Instead, I desperately wanted to replace my awesome 'real job' salary ASAP and get some cash in the bank before I popped out a small human. I needed clients, and I needed them fast.

I took my dodgy-looking website, brushed my ego under the bath mat, and started to pimp myself out as a copywriter.

Now let's get real.

That first year was incredibly tough – boobfeeding while typing, doing client work on 20 minutes' sleep, and arguing with my equally exhausted husband about whose turn it was to do x, y and z.

After a few months I found myself a shared office space, and I'd sneak out one day a week to 'work' there. In reality I just slept at my desk.

It was a daily struggle, but I didn't have any other options. I didn't have my family nearby to babysit, and being the first of my mates to have a baby meant they were all still in party mode.

We had no savings, and were living in expensive rental accommodation in central Sydney.

It was a time of constant guilt about neglecting my mum/wife duties, and constant pressure to earn enough money to keep not just the business going, but also our family.

Okay, this is beginning to sound a little like a rags-to-riches story, so let me qualify.

We were nice, middle-class people who wanted to sustain our nice, middle-class lifestyle. We weren't destitute, and the truth is I always had the option to return to a real job. I wasn't selling broken matches out of a shoe on a rubble-strewn street.

Sitting here writing this, and thinking it was all about the money, has made me realise it wasn't about the money at all.

My business is a lifestyle choice. Back then it was about pride, and not having to go back to corporate life.

My true 'why' was less about 'earning money' and more about 'working from home'.

And it still is.

I don't have a master plan to conquer the world, which may well make me suck as an entrepreneur on paper. But in real life it has served me pretty well.

But things were simpler back then.

In those early days I rarely worried about the competition, and never second-guessed my model. I was too damn busy. I just did the work.

I didn't map out the steps, or set milestones.

I didn't keep myself accountable, or measure myself against objectives.

I just kept on keeping on.

And the rest, as they say, is history. Well, it's my story – the one I'll be telling throughout this book.

Don't wait until you have all your ducks in a row, because by the time you get started some of those ducks will be dead (or at least incredibly elderly).

Even now, after seven years, I'm not entirely sure where all my ducks **are**, let alone how neatly they're lined up.

And if I'd written a business plan, I'm pretty sure it would have been useless after about two weeks.

My business looks **nothing like** the business I started out with. I had no idea what I wanted to do back then or, more importantly, what I was capable of doing.

In all honesty, I think a business plan or even a goal-setting exercise would have either:

- Made me feel bad about all the things I should have been doing but wasn't
- Held me back. (Some of my best business decisions would look incredibly stupid on paper.)

Instead I took (and still take) a more organic approach to business development and planning, and just let things happen.

POINTS TO PONDER

If you like the sound of not writing a business plan, here are some things you'll need instead:

LOVE

It's important to think about what you love. (I've refrained from using 'passion' in this chapter because the word is so overused it makes me gag.)

Because I do believe you must love what you're planning to do.

Yes, you could make a fortune manufacturing fake limbs for pigeons. But do you really love amputee pigeons?

Loving what you do will get you over many a hump, and help you crawl out of several business pits.

SELF-AWARENESS

Is there an aspect of your business that you're not being honest with yourself about?

Being able to take a step back and give yourself a long, hard Paddington Bear-esque stare is an essential skill in both business and life in general.

Whether you're someone who wears their heart (and spleen and kidneys) on your sleeve or are a totally rational beast, you must be able to look at yourself, say, "That was a really stupid idea," and let go of that idea swiftly.

ENDURANCE

Are you truly in this for the long haul, or just to make a quick buck?

Of course, every 'overnight success' you meet will tell you it didn't happen overnight, and that there were many moments of self-doubt and misery.

If you want to get anywhere interesting you need to be able to cling onto the magic business carpet and ride it all the way.

WHAT THEY SAY 

To be a successful entrepreneur you need to map out your journey, plan your steps, assess the risks, and have a backup, growth and exit plan.

WHAT I SAY 

Plan, schplan!

Here's an analogy for you. (You'll soon learn that I'm a big fan of analogies.)

Before heading out on a potentially rainy day you could spend a few hours putting on wellies and extra thick socks. You could also take a raincoat, a hat, and one of those massive golf umbrellas.

Yes, you'll be completely prepared. But by the time you're finally ready to head out it's too late to make it to the park, your enthusiasm has waned, and to top it off it doesn't even rain.

Or you could just wing it. By all means, shove an anorak in your backpack. But then get out there and enjoy a potentially sunny day. And if you do get soaked... well, just enjoy jumping gleefully in puddles.

It sounds a tad glib, but I find everything usually works out in the end. And no amount of careful planning will guarantee success or avert disaster.

These days I try to judge everything I do on three criteria:

- Am I enjoying it?
- Does it make me money?
- Is there a market for it?

I don't even need to check all three boxes. If I'm enjoying what I'm doing but it's making me very little money, I might keep chugging away. And yes, I've occasionally done things I didn't like because people wanted it and it was earning me big bucks.

But if I love something, I go for it. And that love shows through, and tends to make it a success.

CHAPTER 3
I KNOW YOU DON'T LIKE ME AND THAT'S OKAY

One of the hardest things about running your own business is that it's all on you.

There's no boss or team of minions to hide behind. It's just little old you as the face and mouth of your business.

And deciding how to present yourself can be incredibly tough.

At first I got it all wrong.

When I started my business I saw many other copywriters wearing fluffy jumpers, smiling winningly at the camera, and writing lovely, jolly posts about colons.

So I did the same.

I pumped out vanilla posts about nothing much, created kitten-based, inspirational memes, was extraordinarily nice to clients (even when they drove me crazy), and never expressed a strong opinion about anything.

And I took everything so personally. I was devastated when a client didn't like what I'd produced. Horrified if a business relationship didn't work out. And when someone made a nasty comment about a Facebook update, I was crushed.

But then I realised that not everyone is going to love what I do, and that by trying to be all things to all people I was making myself miserable.

Now I'm much more confident about my business style, how I run things, and how I communicate.

Those who know me personally would probably say I'm brutally honest, have an odd sense of humour, am fairly generous, and work faster than a hamster on crack.

So I decided to embrace the me-ness of me.

It didn't happen overnight. But I started to gradually slip more of the everyday phrases I use (I like to call them 'Toonisms') into my writing.

I remember the first time I used the phrase 'bum-clenchingly awesome' in a post for the Australian small business website Flying Solo. It was a risk. It was a bit odd. But the reaction was super positive. In fact, it was one of the first times I had people personally emailing me to say how much they loved my writing style.

Because it finally **was** my writing style – not someone else's.

And over time I began to be more like myself throughout my business.

I'm not particularly fluffy, serious or sophisticated.

I'm honest, quirky and enthusiastic.

So my emails became more straightforward. My opinions more 'out there'. My sense of humour more obvious.

Don't get me wrong. I know my approach isn't everyone's cup of chai.

I know many people won't like my carToony style of branding.

I know the scruffy way I present myself on social media won't appeal to those who prefer a smoother approach.

I know many, **many** people don't like me and the way I do business.

I've been through my fair share of client break-ups. I've suffered from seriously nasty social media comments. I've even survived a negative SEO campaign.

And a few months back someone unsubscribed from my email list because of my 'potty mouth'.

But I'm 100% cool with that because I'm running a business, not a popularity contest.

Here's another home truth: If you try to be someone you're not, you won't attract your kind of people. So if you put yourself out there as some big furry balled sales bitch, then you're going to attract customers who want that kind of attitude from you day in and day out.

It's truly exhausting trying to be something you're not.

I believe succeeding at what you do means realising that some people are just not that into you, and that's okay.

We're told time and again that the key to good online marketing is to 'be yourself'.

But I think being authentic is also the key to running a successful business. Your 'you-ness' should flow through everything you do, from first contact through to final invoice.

POINTS TO PONDER

If you're wondering how to embrace your 'you-ness', here are a few tips:

START SLOWLY

If you've been hiding your crazy personality under a veneer of normality, don't suddenly drop your business pants and start running around naked. Instead, reveal a little bit more of the inner you each day. Think of it as a personality striptease.

KNOW YOUR LIMITS

Rants about politics or religion on your social media page may do you more harm than good. Choose your topics and your moments carefully. Always remain professional. While a touch of quirk is fine, downright craziness won't win you business.

BE SELF-AWARE

Take legitimate criticism on board, and realise that haters are gonna hate. The more of yourself you bring to your business, the more vulnerable you can become. So it's important to build up a big blob of internal confidence before you let everything hang out for the world to see.

TAKE ACTION

Can you identify one bit of **YOU-NESS** you can start including in your business from today onwards?

- Your love of vintage tea cosies?
- Your previous obsession with ballroom dancing?
- The fact that you can play the recorder with your nose?

Try to think about whatever quirk you have that helps make you YOU, and start sharing it with the world.

Psst: If your quirk is something dark and disturbing, consider keeping it to yourself.

WHAT THEY SAY 

Always put your best foot forward, be your best self, and be positive. No one wants to hear about your problems unless you can show how you turned them into a fabulous financial success. Be a winner, be likeable, and smile, SMILE, SMILE!!

WHAT I SAY 

In business, just as in life, most of us quickly realise that not everyone is going to like us. Just as some kids didn't want you on their football team at school, some clients might not want to work with you in business.

And after a while that fixed smile will become an insincere grimace.

Being myself has made running my business far less stressful and far more enjoyable. I am who I am, and my customers can take it or leave it.

I've learned to love my own voice and not give two hoots if others don't. I have a much thicker skin, but don't worry. I'm still squishy on the inside. Like an obese armadillo.

CHAPTER 4
UNDERSTANDING YOUR SUPERPOWERS

I was never a child prodigy.

I didn't grow up being excellent at gymnastics. (You should see me trying to do a forward roll.)

I can't really play any instruments except the recorder with my nose.

And while I can say "I love you because you're a tall and handsome man" in Cantonese, my language skills are a bit rubbish.

I've never been **really** good at anything. Just okayish at a lot of things. If I were a superhero I'd have an 'M' on my cape for Mediocre Woman! (And no, I'm not being self-deprecating here. I love me. But I also know my strengths and weaknesses.)

But looking at some entrepreneurs out there in social media land you'd think you need a superpower to succeed, whether it's inventing your own brand of yoghurt when you were eight or having a chain of poodle massage shops by age 22.

We've been sold the idea that to be a success you need to be horrendously attractive, a chino-wearing supernerd, or someone with a beard. (I'm 99% convinced Branson would be nothing if he was clean shaven.)

Oh, and it also helps if you're bald.

I'm none of these things. But I quickly realised it was important to appreciate my superpowers, however boring and pathetic they seemed.

(Yes, I know 'appreciating my superpowers' might sound a bit 'woo woo'. But bear with me.)

We all have superpowers. And if we can identify them, they can really help make our business a success.

When I started, I felt my superpowers were purely organisational. I could:

- Manage multiple projects and timelines – those agency years served me well
- Create smashing processes and templates – I've always had a strong inner project manager
- Type like a maniac – I'm a 95 wpm ninja[8] on the keyboard

But I didn't feel like a particularly creative or clever copywriter, which was odd seeing as that's how I was positioning myself.

Yes I'd worked in advertising for a while, but only for two years as a copywriter. For the most part I was a producer, and a series of slightly unpleasant Creative Director types had drilled into me that creativity wasn't my strong point.

I had no formal training in writing, and my imposter syndrome was strong. But I wanted to be a copywriter. I felt somewhere inside of me that I was a good writer, and that I could pick up what I needed to know along the way.

And I did.

---

[8] See glossary

I put myself out there as a copywriter for all to see. And I talked the talk before I was confident about walking the walk.

No, I didn't beef up my LinkedIn profile with fake clients.

No, I didn't oversell my abilities.

And no, I didn't charge the big bucks.

I simply called myself a copywriter in a quiet but firm voice. (It took years for me to be confident enough to shout it from the rooftops.)

But even though I wasn't 100% confident in my writing abilities, it didn't matter.

Seriously, it didn't.

Because I quickly realised that while being able to write and type fast were important skills, they weren't the superpowers I really needed to succeed in my chosen field.

I personally know hundreds of great copywriters who aren't doing as well as they'd like to be. But while they're probably better copywriters than I am, maybe they don't possess my *other* superpowers.

MY TRUE SUPERPOWERS

I've thought about this long and hard, and here's what I think my true superpowers **really** are:

1. **Having a good sense of humour** – I may not be laugh-out-loud hysterical, but being able to see the funny side of things certainly helps me get through the day.

2. **Being approachable and friendly** – The more people like working with me, the more work they'll give me. Simple, huh?

3. **Being relatable** – While I may be a touch socially awkward in person, I find it easy to build connections with others online. I

believe this has been a crucial part of growing my audience. I get them, and they get me.

4. **Being a hard worker** – I put the time in and keep going, even when it's a struggle.

5. **Being brave** – I'm not afraid to try new things, fall flat on my bum cheeks, and get up smiling. I'm also not afraid to ask for help when I need it.

WHY RECOGNISING YOUR SUPERPOWERS IS IMPORTANT

Superpowers can become part of your branding, your values, and even your tone of voice.

Branding gurus often say a good way to understand a brand is to think of a person who'd represent it. It's a fun game to play – thinking about who'd play you in a movie (for me I think Kathy Bates in Misery), and who'd be your brand ambassador in an ad (I'd go for Nigella Lawson).

Discovering your superpowers, and then owning them, can make it easier to market yourself and be authentic in everything you do. So be yourself in business, and enjoy it.

BATTLING IMPOSTER SYNDROME

We all suffer from imposter syndrome. Every. Single. One. Of. Us.

Over the past few years I've met oodles of fabulously successful entrepreneurs and business types. And pretty much all of them admit to feeling like a fake from time to time.

Here's an example: I met a super well-known guy at a workshop – one of those entrepreneurs whose face is everywhere, speaks at every event, wins award after award, and gets interviewed by every possible publication.

I took an instant dislike to him. I found him too loud and too full of himself. At the dinner table he held forth with story after story that subtly upped himself as an awesome human being. The ultimate humble bragger.

So I decided to ignore him, and carried on my merry way.

But the fate hedgehogs intervened, and we ended up having to spend a serious lump of time together. We got talking and – surprise, surprise – the confidence was a cover. He was worried about his business, unsure of his direction, and procrastinating with his projects. From the outside it looked like his ducks were totally together, but in actual fact his ducks were all a bit flat and unhappy.

He was just like me. It was a huge relief, and a great reminder that everyone is human and you can never be sure what's going on behind the scenes.

But his super power was that, even with all those worries and self-doubts, he just kept on going. He was doing amazing things despite not being 100% sure of himself.

Knowing your strengths can help you accept your weaknesses.

What do I mean? Well let me tell you a story.

At school Hannah Brandon had bigger boobs than me. And as a blossoming teen it was all about the boobs. Boobs endowed the bearer with greater status, more social power and, most importantly, more admiration from boys.

Us poor boobless creatures were stricken with envy. How could we compare to these full-bosomed creatures? Why were we so pubescently challenged?

I spent many, MANY months wanting to be Hannah Brandon, and trying to emulate her style in every way I could. And yes, this involved taping balls of cotton wool onto the inside of my vest.

Now this might not seem relevant to running a successful business, but hear me out.

It's another one of those metaphor thingies. (And for any males reading this, I'm sure you can think of a substitute appendage for 'boobs'.)

We've all envied someone else's business boobs now and then.

Even now, as an ample-boobed, fully grown businesswoman, the gaping pit of comparison occasionally sucks me in.

I still have a tendency to compare my inadequacies with other people's successes. And I know a lot of other soloists who do the same. So I've included my tips on how to avoid the comparison trap and learn to love your own business – however flat-chested it may be.

It's okay that I'm not slim and glamorous because I'm clever and funny. The good balances out the bad. And I've found that focusing on my superpowers makes me feel better about my (most likely imagined) flaws, which might also work for you.

POINTS TO PONDER

It can be incredibly hard to identify your own superpowers. If you're anything like me, applying positive words to yourself seems somewhat arrogant. So here are some ideas on how you can identify your superpowers more easily:

STEP 1: ASK YOUR FRIENDS

It's totes awkward I know, but take a few minutes to post a Facebook status update along the lines of, *"I'm working on a little personal project, and was wondering if you could think of three words to describe me".*

I went through this process myself and was really surprised by the answers. One word that came up again and again was 'honest', and although it's something I hoped I was, it isn't a word I would have openly applied to myself.

STEP 2: SURVEY YOUR CUSTOMERS

Send a short questionnaire to your customers using something like Survey Monkey to ask them how they feel about you, your business and your products or services. Ask them "What three words best describe my service?"

STEP 3: REALLY READ YOUR TESTIMONIALS

If you're in the habit of collecting testimonials for your work (which you should be), take some time to read them carefully. Highlight any adjectives you find, and add them to your superpower list.

STEP 4: LOOK AT YOUR CUSTOMERS

Take a good look at the customers you're attracting to your business. How would you describe them? Do you like them? Would you invite them over for a glass of wine and a crumpet?[9]

Often we attract people similar to us, so try looking at the qualities **they** have and see if they also apply to you.

Once you've tried all of these methods, create a list of commonly used words and see how they sit with you. They may be your hidden superpowers. You may even discover some you never knew you had.

Embrace them. Own them. And start applying them to everything you do.

And if you're stuck in the comparison trap and can't clamber out, here are some tips that will help:

Stop hate following

We all have those competitors who lodge themselves in the back of our brain. We subscribe to their newsletters and 'like' their Facebook pages not because we love them, but because we're jealous of everything they do.

We open their emails with a groan, and mutter expletives under our breath as we see the latest 'shiny thing' they've just done or new opportunity they've been offered.

Unsubscribing from their emails and removing their pages from your newsfeed will make you a happier chipmunk.

Start producing

Instead of reading other people's content and checking out their blogs, websites and emails, start creating your **own** content. Rather than following others, listen to your **own** customers and let them guide you towards new products, services and solutions.

---

[9] If you're not a fan of crumpets, replace with posh crisps like Hedgehog and Balsamic Vinegar Favor Stone Washed Kettle Chips.

Once you don your business blinkers your vision will clear, making it easier for you to come up with your own ideas.

Be realistic

If you're just starting out, there's little joy in comparing yourself with a well-established business. As the saying goes, don't compare your beginning to someone else's middle, or your behind-the-scenes with their highlights reel.

Don't believe the hype

I've met many of my business heroes and peers, and the truth is a lot of them are struggling. Everyone has their ups and downs in business, but not everyone reveals them on social media.

Remember that most business folk are putting a brave, successful face on things. When it comes to business marketing, there's a certain amount of bra stuffing going on (if you catch my drift).

WHAT THEY SAY 

Work to your strengths, be confident, and never show that you're struggling with insecurity.

And never compare. If you're busy looking at who is to the side and behind you, you'll never win the race. Play your own game, and do your own thing.

WHAT I SAY 

While I agree with what 'they' say, their advice is almost impossible to follow.

Many business owners struggle with a negative mindset and a lack of confidence. And sometimes knowing everyone else feels the same way isn't enough. We've got to turn that frown upside down and learn to see our inner awesomeness.

When the fog of business comparison starts to rise, try to remember your successes. Spend some time reading old client testimonials, and take stock of your achievements so far. I keep a folder of 'nice things' (comments, pictures, reviews etc.) on my desktop to trawl through when I'm feeling inadequate. It's simple but effective.

Running a business can be a lonely old game. It's important to be honest with yourself, and realise that 99% of people are probably feeling the same way you do.

In fact, there's probably a businessperson out there right now looking at your success and gnashing their teeth with envy. Remember, there are people out there who will love your business (and your boobs, for that matter) regardless of its size or impressiveness.

So don't let them pass you by while you're busy comparing yourself to others. Instead, go forth and find your superpowers, people. You'll be glad you did.

CHAPTER 5

MORE BUSTLE THAN HUSTLE

ENTREPRENEURIAL REQUIREMENT

A love of selling

If there's one thing a true entrepreneur needs to be, it's a natural salesperson.

If you can't sell sand to the Arabs, snow to the Eskimos, or stationery to the copywriters, then why the hell are you thinking about starting your own business?

Well, let me tell you that if there's one thing I'm rubbish at (other than rollerskating), it's selling.

I hate to sell.

The very idea of it makes me itchy.

Yes, as a kid I was the one with the lemonade stand. Actually, being British meant it was a Ribena stand set up in our driveway. And my only customers were Mum, Dad and my brother. But I enjoyed the thrill of selling back then.

I even started my own membership club when I was around eight years old – "The monkey club". And when you joined you got a membership card, a weekly magazine and a badge.

Admittedly only one issue of the magazine was ever published. (Even back then I knew print media was dead.) But my three members (thanks again Mum, Dad and Chris) paid their weekly subscription for a few more months, and I was hooked on the whole passive income thing.

It wasn't until adulthood that my sales phobia began.

As a student, money was tight. I still remember taking my 11 pence (around 20 cents) to the corner shop and begging for a single egg and half an onion to make 'omelette à la Toon' (still a personal favourite).

So when the chance to earn a commission selling aerial photographs came up, I jumped at the chance.

Or rather, grunted "Okay" while levering myself from the throw-covered saggy sofa in our tatty student flat.

They drove a group of us to an anonymous estate on the outskirts of Liverpool, where we were given an aerial photograph of our appointed cul-de-sac and told to go forth and sell. (By this stage all the nice posh housing estates had already been ticked off the list.)

The hugely expensive photos displayed rows and rows of drab grey roofs in sad, treeless streets. I remember identifying one person's house by the tiny burning sofa in the photo, the burnt-out shell of which their eight children were now using as a trampoline.

It was tough work. Most people immediately slammed the door in my face. Others talked to me for hours, but clearly had no intention of buying. They were just lonely.

The photos weren't even very good – blurry shots in ugly, overpriced frames.

In two weeks I sold just one photo to an old couple. But the brief moment of elation (I'd finally earned a £20 commission) was quickly squashed by a feeling of disgust knowing they clearly couldn't afford it.

I chucked the job in the next day. And I learned that it's really hard to sell a crap product you don't believe in.

But what if you **do** believe in your product? What if you're genuinely happy with what you do, and feel it could truly help other people? It should be super easy to sell then, right?

Wrong.

As a copywriter I could list out sales page formulas until the cows, sheep and pigs came home. And yet when it came to creating that kind of copy for myself, I often struggled.

I know full well that things like tripwires, sales funnels, long sales letters and irritating pop-ups can work wonders sales-wise. But they still felt pushy and uncomfortable to me.

Well, at least until I stopped trying to sell the way I was "supposed" to.

I realised I didn't need to exaggerate, oversell and write 9000-word sales letters. I could get my product out there by being a human talking to other humans – just as I would if I met them face to face.

I stopped trying to up-sell and cross-sell.

In fact, I pretty much stopped trying to sell altogether, and began to explain instead.

ASKING THE BIG QUESTIONS

Of course, I'd had service sales pages on my copywriting site for years. But when I started selling products, memberships and courses, it felt different. It felt harder.

So I asked myself some simple questions:

- What problem am I trying to solve?
- How does my 'thing' solve it?

- What are the alternatives to my thing, and why aren't they as good?
- What does my thing actually do?
- How does my thing benefit the person using it?
- How does my thing make that person feel?

And after everything I wrote I asked myself the question, "So what?"

"So what?" is a powerful question that makes you evaluate everything you write and say.

For example:

- "More than 2,500 people have taken my ecourse." So what? Well, if that many people trusted their purchase decision, new customers can too.
- "The course includes eight coaching calls" So what? Customers are not just left going solo, they get support and can feel more confident while learning.

By answering the 'So what?' question, you're pushing your sales copy harder as well as proving why your product or service really is worth buying.

THE POWER OF PROOF

It's simple: Other people can say things about you and your products that you can't say yourself without sounding like an arrogant idiot.

One of my biggest lessons along the way has been the power of word-of-mouth recommendations, whether it's in person, in writing or on video.

I work harder at getting testimonials than I do pretty much everything else.

BEING REAL

We're always being told to be ourselves. I know it sounds trite, but it wasn't until I started being me – talking like I normally do, and letting my great sense of humour and poor sense of fashion show through – that I truly felt comfortable placing my goods on the virtual sales counter.

I don't need to have a smooth sales spiel.

I just talk like I would to a friend. I don't make big promises. I don't exaggerate. I share my highs and my lows.

By the time someone buys a product from me they generally feel like they know me.

And all of that builds trust.

If someone trusts you they're buying the person, not the thing. And for many of us small business folk, we are synonymous with our business. The more you're willing to get yourself 'out there' and be yourself, the easier you'll find the whole selling process.

THE ACCIDENTAL FUNNEL

In Chapter 7 I'll be taking you through my approach to learning. But for the sake of this chapter I'm going to reveal one piece of information now.

I have never taken an online course.

All those amazing sales funnel strategies? I don't know 'em.

(Psst if you don't know what a sales funnel is, check out the glossary at the end of this book.)

That awesome sales method? I haven't read about it.

And yet I still manage to sell – a lot.

Why? Because most of it is common sense.

Lure people in with something free. Make sure it's really good – better than what someone else is charging for.

Then try to sell them something a little bigger.

And then something a little bigger again.

And then try to sell them the big, big thing.

It's not rocket science.

Keep the pricing just as simple

Selling something that's expensive often takes more work than selling something that's relatively cheap. But not always. Selling a $5 checklist can be as hard as selling a $10k mastermind package if you haven't got the customer's trust.

People like to feel like they're getting a bargain.

People like bundles and offers.

People don't like round numbers. (That's why $997 looks a lot cheaper than $1000.)

People like to feel special.

People want to feel confident in their purchase choice.

But above all else...

KEEPING IT REAL ON FACEBOOK

I see so many businesses getting it wrong on Facebook. Endlessly pumping out self promotional piddle and wondering why no one cares.

The worst place for it is the Facebook groups, where people look for any opportunity to push their own business agenda.

Most conversations in FB groups go something like this.

Person 1: Vague question, which is really self promotion.

Person 2: Generous answer, which is really self promotion.

Person 3: Short confused answer, ending in LOL

Person 4: F[10]

Person 5: Serious answer, tagging someone else.

Person 6: Tagged person writes a 600-word essay.

Person 5: You are so great tagged person

Person 7: Argues with person 6.

Person 6: Argues back.

Person 7: Gets personal

Person 6: Uses statistics

Admin: Encourages love and understanding.

Person 3: Still don't get it. LOL

Person 7: Leaves group

Person 8: Irrelevant comment.

Person 9: Asks question that has already been answered 3 times but is too lazy to read.

Person 10: I've pmed you hun.

Person 6: Follows up with another 600 word essay.

Person 1: Thanks everyone, (hasn't read comments) then provides link to their thing.

<2 weeks pass>

Person 3: Lol.

<2 months pass>

Person 11: F

---

[10] For those who don't know, 'F' means follow, and people type it into Facebook chat streams so they'll get notifications. But Facebook actually has a feature that lets you be notified without annoying everyone who has already commented.

Of course I may or may not have been persons 1-11. But these days my approach to Facebook is to 'seek first to help'. I dedicate time each week to answering questions, giving advice and tips. At first I did this in other groups, then I created my own.

And while I do still do promotional posts, I'd say they make up about 2% of my overall Facebook interaction.

PEOPLE WANT TO BUY FROM PEOPLE

Now we've all heard this before. But what does it actually mean?

To me, it means you have to step out from behind your desk and into the spotlight.

You have to be the face and the voice of your business.

You have to turn up, contribute, help, discuss and explain.

No amount of sexy sales copy will ever beat a conversation. So have as many conversations as you can – in person, online, in webinars, in Facebook Live sessions, in groups, and wherever else you can manage.

Once people get to know you I'm sure they'll love you. And when they love you they'll want to buy your stuff.

POINTS TO PONDER

59

If you're creating sales material, here are some ideas that have worked well for me.

SELL BY HELPING

I spend a lot of time in Facebook groups offering advice and answering questions. And most of the time I do it without even mentioning my products and services.

I don't immediately send the person a private message trying to flog my wares. I wait to be asked. And if they don't ask, then I don't tell.

Some people will be ungrateful. You may even find yourself in a 'help comments war' from time to time. But more often than not you'll also make a genuine connection with that person.

And don't forget those who quietly read your advice and find their way to you.

SELL BY GIVING

Every time I launch a new product or service, I start by giving it away. Not to millions, but to a select few. I do it mainly to test out my product and get invaluable feedback on what I need to change. But in doing so I receive some added benefits – people's gratitude, involvement and positive (and often public) thanks.

I'm not into the culture of 'everything for free'. I think it can become a really slippery slope for many business owners (especially females). But a sprinkle of free now and again can be a useful weapon in your armoury.

TOOT YOUR OWN HORN

"I hate talking about myself," they cry.

"I don't want to sound arrogant," they whisper.

"No one wants to hear my story," they mumble.

The truth is, people love to hear about other people's successes, however small. You don't want your media sharing to be all "Me, me me" of course. But there's nothing wrong with celebrating your wins. And one of the most powerful ways of doing this is to use other people's words. This makes getting testimonials a top priority.

ALWAYS ASK FOR A TESTIMONIAL.

You may get a "No". But you may also get an amazing comment that not only gives you confidence, but that you can share – everywhere.

Give the person writing the testimonial a bit of a structure to work with, a little template they can fill in quickly and easily:

"Kate is an <TBC> copywriter. We chose her because <REASON>. We found the best thing about working with Kate was <SOMETHING>."

WHAT THEY SAY 

Create consumer avatars, map out your sales funnel, and identify your customers' touch points.

WHAT I SAY 

Be human, and be real. Don't try so hard to create convoluted strategies and funnels. Just think like a customer and be genuine.

CHAPTER 6
SLIGHTLY FRAZZLED

A client once asked for a meeting in the city.

When he met me, he looked me up and down and said, "Honestly, I wouldn't meet people in person. Better to keep up the illusion of your profile photo".

This was back in the days when I had a heavily Photoshopped vintage snap from the guys at Sherbet Birdie as my profile shot. Yep, just like that sexy as hell one on the cover.

This bloke's comments cut me to the quick. But the truth is… well, it was the truth.

I looked nothing like my photo. It was a lie. Even when I looked like that I never looked like **that.**

No-one looks like that.

But it was a lie I was happy to hide behind because I didn't want anyone to know how I really looked.

It brought back memories of my first proper job.

My boss called me into her office for a serious chat.

"Do you think you look smart?" she asked.

I looked down at my business attire.

"Yes," I answered nervously.

"Well, you don't," she replied.

Admittedly she was slathered in enough make-up to cover a cow. But she was still my boss, and her opinion mattered to me.

That conversation has always stuck with me.

I just don't do corporate glam well. Not then, and not now.

For a long time it held me back from getting my face out there for my brand.

My insecurities whispered that unless I was 20 kilos lighter with bigger boobs and a glossy mane, no-one would take me seriously and buy from me.

And looking at most of the super successful entrepreneurs, you'd be forgiven for thinking it too.

Of course, there's always some famous American entrepreneur who usually looks like he's just woken up in a bin after a hard night of clubbing. (I won't mention any names – you can work it out for yourself.)

But the rest of them all look so polished. That light tan, the hair that doesn't move, the aggressively white teeth and perfectly tailored suits.

The women cross their legs in chairs, never worrying about positioning themselves to avoid calf flab. And the men never seem to worry about double chins – even the ones **with** double chins.

Maybe they're earning enough money to pay for private chefs and personal trainers.

Maybe they have a team of make-up artists that help them look their best for each video.

Maybe they're all just impossibly hot.

But I'm **not** crazy hot. And for a long time I felt that because I wasn't, I couldn't be an entrepreneur.

You might be thinking that I have my crap together. Yes, I have a few photos where I look okay. And I look quite glam in some of my videos.

But you don't see me frantically dry shampooing my fringe, or plucking my yeti brows seconds before I start. You don't know how long I spend blurring out lumps and bumps before I share that casual selfie.

I know it's nothing new, but I've never been super confident about my looks. And chances are you don't like the way you look either, or have a pet hate about your appearance.

But as a 42-year-old woman I've obviously learned to deal with it in day-to-day life.

I don't care how I look when I'm walking the dog, posting letters or buying a Thai takeaway. My husband thinks I look okay, as does my son, and my dog thinks I'm gorgeous. That's enough for me.

But putting your face to your business is a whole different kettle of quiche.

In Chapter 4 I talked about having to accept that not everyone will like the way you run your business. And over the years I've developed a thick skin to shield me from the comments about my tone of voice, my methods and my approach.

But for some reason I take criticisms about how I look a lot harder.

I'm under no illusion that some people judge me on how I look – men and women. I know they make purchase decisions, recommendations and conclusions based on the way I look.

And it irks me hugely because looking glam isn't something that comes naturally to me. To be honest, looking even half-decent isn't something that comes naturally to me.

As a child I was a tomboy growing up who adored my big brother. I'm not good at hair and make-up. My mum is naturally attractive, and so never taught me how to perfectly apply lipstick. And at school I was never friends with the girly girls.

I like to think I have great taste in clothes, but I'm pretty sure I don't.

At first, I tried to fake it.

I made a video for one of my sales pages, modelled on a well-known business entrepreneur. I even clipped in false straight hair extensions. I slathered on inches of make-up, set up my lighting kit, positioned my ring light and made my video.

And it was totally not me. I hated it.

So I changed my mindset. Ugh! Did I actually just use the word mindset? Shame on me.

Yes, I'm a bit chubby. I will never have sleek hair. And I may not be everyone's cup of tea looks-wise.

But I don't make my purchasing decisions based on looks. And I'd rather have customers like me than be all judgey wudgey.

Giving up on having the 'right' look has given me an immense feeling of freedom. And on the few occasions people do comment on my slightly frazzled appearance, it's about how it makes me seem more real. And because I can do 'the thing' while being scruffy, it means they can too.

POINTS TO PONDER

If you're struggling to embrace your face, here are some tips that might make it easier:

THINK ABOUT IT

Do you ever buy something because of how someone looks? I'm betting you base your purchasing decision more how the person treated you. You may even find the super-glam shop assistants a bit intimidating, and the ones who look a little less polished more approachable.

Well, guess what? The same applies to business.

BE YOUR BEST SELF

While it's important to be content with your looks, it's also good to be your best self. Consider getting a haircut the day before you record a set of videos. Take a few minutes to pop on some make-up before you do a Facebook Live chat. (Yep, that goes for you blokes as well. Just grab a simple concealer or something.) Brush your teeth. Pluck your nose hairs. And wear a clean top.

LIGHTS. CAMERA. ACTION

When it comes to taking a good snap or making a good video, lighting is everything. You can buy a cheap lighting kit on eBay for a few hundred dollars. Later on you may even want to invest in a ring light to give your eyes some sparkle.

BE COMFORTABLE

When you're making videos, appearing in person or having a photo shoot, wear something you feel comfortable in. Forget about wearing those new shoes or trying out that new outfit – you'll just feel awkward. And believe me, it will show.

BE YOURSELF

It sounds trite, but being yourself is so important.

If your photographer asks for a big smile, but you're more of a slight grin type of person, go with the slight grin. If you're struggling with video making, imagine you're explaining the topic to a good friend. And of course, always imagine that your audience at that big speaking event is either naked or sitting on the loo. Or even both.

WEAR 'THE' OUTFIT

You know the one. The outfit that always gets you compliments. The one you **know** you look and/or feel great in. Who cares if it isn't smart suit that **other** entrepreneurs wear. Just do your own thing and you'll be fine.

WHAT THEY SAY 

Sex and good looks sell. The better you look, the more your business will thrive.

WHAT I SAY 

Even naturally scruffy people can do simple things to present themselves nicely.

You don't need to look polished and straight off a magazine cover like all those 'real entrepreneurs'. And you don't have to go all Marie Forleo* in your videos.

But you **can** be true to your inner 'scruffiness' while still being professional. Just remember to keep a can of dry shampoo by your desk.

* If you don't know who Marie Forleo is, give her a quick Google. She has a ridiculous amount of awesome hair.

CHAPTER 7
LEARNING BY DOING

When I started out I had zero business experience. My degree in Roman history and Renaissance poetry meant I could list every emperor and quote John Donne. But I had no idea how to manage cashflow or generate sales.

And my career in ad agencies didn't give me any clues, either. At work I just turned up, did the thing, drank the free wine and went home again. Even when they encouraged us to fill out timesheets and care about our clients we weren't **really** kept accountable. If we failed miserably, it was always the head of someone higher up that ended up on the chopping block.

So when I decided to start my own business it probably would have been a good idea to take a business course. Or at least head to Amazon for a book on how to be a killer entrepreneur.

Millions of humans have run businesses before, and there are oodles of self-made entrepreneurs. So why not learn from their experiences?

Sadly, the thought never even occurred to me. I don't know why. It just didn't.

Today the interweb is full of e-courses on everything from 'How to manage Facebook ads' to 'How to clean your piglets'.

But back then we didn't have anything like that. Or if we did, then I certainly didn't know about them.

Mind you, even if I **did** know about them I probably wouldn't have bought any.

You see, I'm rather stingy. Not about giving to others, but about investing in myself. I love seeing money coming in, and it physically hurts seeing money going out. I mean it. It actually hurts. For reelz. (Unless of course it's late night shopping for new frocks or my renewing Netflix subscription.)

So whenever I see those Entrepreneur Mastermind courses I just think, "No, I'm not paying to learn your formula. I want to make my **own** formula".

Even now I struggle to buy things for my business. I'll have 'the thing' in my cart for weeks before I finally submit.

Here's something else about me: I'm a curious beast.

I like knowing how to do 'the thing' – getting 'under the hood' and seeing how it all works. Partly because I'm a glutton for learning, and partly because I'm scared of being ripped off because I don't know enough about 'the thing' to avoid it.

And business books? I'm really not a fan, which is ironic given that I'm writing one. But honestly I'd rather read some historical non-fiction or a gripping thriller than dive into 'How to boost Your LinkedIn Profile in 827 Easy Steps.'

I could also have sold a kidney to pay for a business coach. But in the eight years I've worked in my business I've yet to find one who resonates with me[11].

---

[11] Apart from Robert Gerrish, of course, who kindly wrote the foreword for this book. Fortunately the occasional chats I have with him are free because he's such a good bloke and because I know all his secrets.

So when I started out I did everything myself. And I'm still pretty much a DIYer.

In those early years I barely invested a penny in my business beyond the $80 I spent on 200 business cards. (And after posting one to my mum, forcing my husband to take another, and putting one in my wallet. I still have 197 left. Want one?)

As I mentioned in Chapter 1, my mate at work built my blog for me. At that stage I wasn't even sure what a blog was. But it was a nifty little WordPress-hosted site that I could edit myself, so I was happy.

From there I:

- Wrote my own copy (obviously)
- Managed my accounts on a tired Excel spreadsheet
- Designed my own email templates
- Managed my own social media

It was pretty much just me, myself and I. And none of us had any idea what we were doing.

I started out using the processes I'd learned working in ad agencies, running my business motorbike on the petrol of agency life until I was driving on fumes.

I sent LinkedIn connections to anyone and everyone I knew, including people I'd brushed past once in a corridor in 1998. I was a total LinkedIn whore.

I also emailed all my mates and offered to do 'stuff' for nothing. And I offered to do pretty much anything: website building, email setups, functional specifications, press releases, and even some **really** terrible design work.

And the pattern was always the same. First I'd get the job, and then I'd work out how to do the job.

But I worked hard, learned hard, and the result weren't bad. The clients were happy. And in those early years I managed to stuff a sock in the mouth of my inner perfectionist.

I learned by doing. I learned from my mistakes and my successes.

Was that the best way? Probably not.

I look at people starting business today and envy the resources they have at their fingertips. I look at the templates, courses and community I offer at **The Clever Copywriting School** and envy my own customers.

How much easier would it have been if I'd just read one damn book?

I undoubtedly wasted countless hours learning the hard way. But I also think the information began to 'stick' a lot faster than it would have if I'd read about someone else doing it.

I still think it's the best way to learn, which is why all the courses I teach focus more on the 'How' and the 'Do' than the 'What' and the 'Why'.

So, do you need to invest in a course or a coach, or can you go it alone? Here are five key factors to consider:

1. THE RIGHT TEACHER

The first thing you need is someone to learn from. Ideally they'll have a sockful of experience, a great reputation, and a proven methodology. You can waste a lot of time reading random articles and watching videos when what you **really** need is a simple step-by-step guide – a complete start-to-finish program that takes you through everything.

TOONTIP: While you can pick up bits and bobs of information by reading gazillions of articles, nothing beats having a guided program to learn from.

2. THE RIGHT TOOLS

There are a gazillion apps and software programs out there that can help you do the thing. But the truth is, they won't do the thing for you. You need to learn how to use the tool.

So many business people buy an app or a course and think, "That's it. I'm done." But the truth is they haven't even started. It's like thinking you'll get fit just from buying a running machine. Cray-Cray.

TOONTIP: Some jobs are impossible to do without the right tools. And this is where you have to weigh up the value of doing it yourself. The professional will already have the necessary tools – they're part of what you're paying for. They'll also have years of experience using those tools, and can complete a job that would take you all day in 30 minutes.

3. TIME TO INVEST

Nothing worth learning is worth learning quickly. Or something.

If you're going to do the DIY thing then you'll need to put some time aside to get stuck in, make mistakes, practice and mess around. Don't be fooled into thinking DIY is better than paying someone else. While it will save you money, it will also cost you time.

TOONTIP: If you're truly interested in what you're doing, the time will fly. And if it's something you'll do again and again then it's probably worth the effort. But spending a week mastering Adobe Illustrator just to design one logo might not be such a great idea.

4. COMMON SENSE

Sometimes it makes **much** more sense to outsource. I've attempted and failed many, *many* tasks, and wasted heaps of time and money getting things fixed. Fortunately I'm now much better at judging when I need to stop and learn, and when I need to let it go.

TOONTIP: Knowing your limitations is important. If you start to feel unsure about what you're doing you should stop, take stock and call an expert **before** you cause irrevocable damage.

5. ONGOING SUPPORT

Learning a new skill isn't easy. And it doesn't happen overnight. You can't just shove an instruction manual into someone's hands and expect them to become an instant expert.

We need to double-check our thinking, and have someone to turn to when things don't quite work out as we'd planned.

TOONTIP: Having someone there to answer your questions is a key part of DIY business success. A teacher can give you support and motivation, keep you accountable, and help you cope with overwhelm.

POINTS TO PONDER

If you're wondering whether to shell out for a course, coach or expert to help you with a particular part of your business, these tips might help:

EVALUATE

Look at the task and ask yourself a few questions:

1. Is it something you'll do over and over again, or just once? If it's a one-off job, such as building your website, then think about outsourcing it. But make sure you get training from the developer so you can maintain it yourself if you want to.

2. Is it something you're genuinely interested in? As much as I'm a geek and love learning techie stuff, I don't like things that are **too** techie. That's why I taught myself HTML, but didn't bother learning PHP.

3. Can you afford it? On average, what do you make in an hour? If your hourly rate is way more than the person you're outsourcing to, then it's a win-win. But if it's way less, consider doing it yourself – at least for now.

COMPLETE BEFORE YOU CONTINUE

If you're a bit of an e-course junkie, force yourself to commit. Don't allow yourself to buy another course until you've completed all the ones you've already purchased. Choose wisely, and learn from people you enjoy, admire and could imagine having a glass of wine with. You're going to spend many hours listening to their voices and reading their words.

FIND ANSWERS ELSEWHERE

One of the best decisions I made in my business was to start a series of communities. I set up SEO and copywriting communities, and invited my peers to join. We get to learn from each other, and it saves us all a bundle on expensive courses.

Even now, I have communities for customers and smaller ones I share with my peers so I can keep learning.

WHAT THEY SAY 

If you want a successful business, hire great people and outsource everything so you can focus on what you do best.

WHAT I SAY 

For many, employing businesses to do the thing is a luxury they can't afford, and so DIY is the only option.

I'm a firm believer that any skill can be learned with enough time and determination. But it's also important to look at what you enjoy doing, and how you want to spend your time.

CHAPTER 8
TURNING COMPETITORS INTO CHEERLEADERS

Everyone frets about the competition.

Yes, even those super-successful entrepreneurs.

Whether you're an old established firm terrified about young upstarts, or a new business trying to break into a competitive field, it's hard not to be fearful.

After all, there's only so much business pie to go around, right? And your slice is barely big enough as it is. So how will you cope if your competitors start taking a bite?

Well, I've got a radical suggestion to help you overcome the fear of your competitors: embrace them.

If there's one thing true entrepreneurs do, it's blaze their own path. Now I haven't always succeeded at this, but at least it's on the checklist for me to possibly tick later on.

When I gave up my real job and became a full-time copywriter, I often wondered if the competition would be too much.

If you type 'Copywriter Sydney' or 'SEO copywriter Sydney' into

Google you'll see there are zillions of copywriting businesses out there. So how on earth could I make my mark? And would I ever be able to get enough work?

Well, I managed to make my mark and get enough work to not only establish my business but also keep it going. And here's how I did it, in five simple steps:

STEP 1: IGNORE THE COMPETITION

It's important not to get overwhelmed by everyone else out there.

Think about your own business and your goals, and be **true to your vision.** If you're good at what you do, and you work bloody hard, you'll be right (as the Aussies say).

Or, as they whispered in that Kevin Costner film, Field of Dreams, "If you build it, they will come"[12].

STEP 2: COPY THE COMPETITION

Okay, so it sounds like I'm contradicting Step 1. And I kind of am. But bear with me – it will all make sense soon.

Once you've established your own business idea, and have a clear vision of how you're going to present yourself, check out what your competitors are up to.

Is there anything you can 'borrow'? Do you need to tweak your model/idea a little?

Obviously, copying is bad. But 'being inspired by' someone else is fine.

But it's often hard to define what the differences are between 'copying', 'borrowing' and 'being inspired by'. And I'm not sure I can

---

[12] I know, I know. The line was actually, "If you build it, he will come". But you want more than one client, right?

draw a clean line for you.

Look, if you have two tabs open and you're cutting and pasting, that's bad, okay?

But if you have a quick browse around, then close down the other websites and get down to doing your thing, it's probably okay.

I think you know in your gut if you're stealing. So listen to your gut. It's very wise.

Just remember to always be yourself. Because as the cliché goes, "everyone else is taken".

STEP 3: BEFRIEND THE COMPETITION

I'd argue that my three biggest competitors (in terms of search position) are also my three closest business chums. We regularly get in touch to share each other's blog posts, re-tweet each other's tweets, and ask for help and advice.

We're not precious, and it works.

And it's not just us. There are hordes of copywriters out there in the Twittersphere who also refuse to be precious. It might sound hard to believe, but we're one big happy community of copywriters.

(Cue group hug.)

When I started my first copywriter community about six years ago, I sent emails to around 40 copywriters. (I'll talk more about this later.) Around 25 replied, 14 ignored me, and one turned into a nightmare dickhead stalker who thwarted my existence for about a year. Fun times.

But even with the dickhead, I'd say those are still pretty good odds.

STEP 4: RECOMMEND YOUR COMPETITION

Hopefully you'll reach the point where you have to turn down a job/project because you're too busy. But instead of just saying "No", why not give the potential customer some recommendations?

Simply find a few competitors whose work you admire, and pass on their details. You could even speak to them, and ask them to reciprocate.

Your customers will be grateful for some guidance, your competitors will be grateful for the work, you may potentially have work referred to you down the track – a real win-win-win.

STEP 5: HELP THE COMPETITION

I get several emails a week from up-and-coming copywriters wanting advice. Do I quake in my boots about these Gen Y upstarts coming to snaffle my customers?

No, I don't. Well, not always.

I believe there's enough work for everyone. So I always try to share the love and help people when I can.

From a business point of view, everyone you help could potentially recommend you later on. And from a karmic point of view, you'll be positively glowing.

Now this might all sound a little too lovey-dovey for you. This isn't the stuff of hard-nosed businessmen, and Gordon Gecko definitely wouldn't approve. So if you don't think it's your style then no worries. All I'm saying is that it certainly worked for me.

The combination of working hard and sharing the love with my competitors has been a huge benefit to my business. I'm close to the top of Google for a highly competitive keyword phrase. And with almost 95% of the work I take on coming from recommendations, it feels like the **good vibes** I'm sending out are coming back tenfold.

So instead of fearing your competitors, befriend them. Start killing them with kindness, and slowly you'll turn them into cheerleaders.

POINTS TO PONDER

If you like the sound of turning your competitors into cheerleaders, here are some tips on how to get started:

START A COMMUNITY

Set up a small private Facebook group and email some of your competitors to see if they're interested in joining. Start with something like:

> *"Hi Sue*
>
> *I just wanted to quickly connect and say "Hi". We're both in the <category> industry, and I'm a big admirer of your work. You can check out my business at <your domain name>.*
>
> *I'm a strong believer in the idea that there's enough work to go around, and that so-called competitors can actually be business buddies. That's why I've set up the <name of community> Community.*
>
> *It's a no-fee, easy-going Facebook group where we can openly share ideas, tips and our ups and downs in a non-competitive way.*
>
> *Would you be interested in joining?"*

Of course, this email will go down much better if you've already connected online. Even so, expect a fair number of people to reject your offer. But even if you find only one or two like-minded souls, it could really transform how you see your business, and expand your world a little.

SEND A REFERRAL

Next time you can't complete that job, offer that service or provide that product, refer the customer to your competitor. The customer will admire your openness, as will your competitor. And over time they may start sending some love back your way.

But make sure you do your homework first. Don't just randomly recommend someone, because if they suck it will reflect badly on you.

WHAT THEY SAY 

True entrepreneurs don't focus on the competition. They focus on **beating** the competition. And once they're done they clamber over the bruised and broken bodies of their competitors to reach even greater heights.

WHAT I SAY 

Quite simply, I couldn't have gotten to where I've... er, gotten to without the help of my competitors. I've learned a *huge* amount over the years from other people in the same field. And I've been blown away by the openness and generosity.

My competitors have been my greatest referrers and my best customers. And most importantly, I now consider many of them to be my best friends.

A WORD OF CAUTION

I must finish this chapter with a warning: not all competitors are created equal. In fact, some are created as complete arse hats.

While I've found it increasingly easy to befriend my fellow business owners in the world of copywriting, in the world of Search Engine Optimisation it hasn't always been such a happy story.

I've joined many forums and communities in the male-dominated SEO arena to try and reach out to other SEO lovers.

But it's been a mixed bag.

In many of these groups, asking questions is considered a sign of weakness. Everyone sees you as the dumb-arse gazelle in a crowd of snarky hyenas.

One particular competitor took delight in taking screenshots of my questions from the early days, and then turning them into patronising blog posts where he showed his authority over me by answering them.

I was often picked on in the forums because I was open about my desire to learn. But despite this I found some absolute gems of humans in those groups, many of whom are now guests on my podcast.

So while there may be a few haters out there, I find they're generally drowned out by the awesome folk.

CHAPTER 9
DEALING WITH COPYCATS

Okay, so in the previous chapter I talked about giving all your competitors a big fat squeeze of love.

But sometimes it isn't that easy.

I generally take a pretty chilled approach to running my business, and to competitors. But if there's one thing that really gets my goat, it's copycats.

Now I know that in a previous chapter I talked about how it's fine to look at competitor sites for inspiration. But it needs to stop right there.

Inspiration does not mean copying the page word for word, or replicating the logo, or stealing photos. You need to know the difference.

Copycats are the types who trawl your site and then rip off your ideas, steal your content, and regurgitate your creativity as their own.

Over the years I've been copycatted more times than I care to remember. And as I became slightly more well known, the rate of copycatting increased.

There was the copywriter I helped build a business for, who then unashamedly ripped off huge chunks of my website.

The one who took templates I'd given her freely and started using them as opt-ins on her own website.

And the student who not only launched her own **SEO** course two days after attending mine but also **CALLED IT THE SAME THING.**

I could go on. But it's boring, so I won't.

Over the years I've been the victim of a thousand thefts – some subtle, others blatant.

I should be flattered. But the truth is, it seriously shits me. And having talked to other small business types, I know copycats piss you off too.

Here's how I've learned to cope:

UNDERSTAND TRENDS

If you find huge chunks of your words on another website, that's straight out copycatting. But what about when someone copies your style, idea or concept?

It's hard to define, and even harder to prove.

One is the recent trend of hand-written fonts, which I first discovered via Liss Letters when she made a rather lovely downloadable thingy for my website.

But pretty soon everyone had what looked like hand-written fonts. And then gold stuff came into vogue, and suddenly gold copy and gold graphics were everywhere.

Everyone looked like copycats. But who copied who?

Even Kmart started daubing pen pots and pillows with golden handwritten fonts. Did Kmart copy us too?

What looks like copycatting is often just a trend. Be careful of who you accuse.

LEARN ACCEPTANCE

The truth is, copycatting is just part of running a business.

While you can trademark and claim copyright, it probably won't protect you unless you're willing to file an expensive lawsuit.

As the old adage goes, "Pioneers get arrows in their backs". So learn to accept the copycatting, and develop a thick(er) skin.

CONFRONT THE COPYCAT

If you're certain your content has been ripped off, feel free to call out your copycat. Just be polite, succinct and honest, and you'll be okay.

One copycat stole an entire sales page from my site, making only subtle changes. When I confronted him about it he apologised, saying that while he'd used my content for inspiration he hadn't realised how close it was to the original. He promised to change it.

Sadly, he never did. But I still felt better for confronting him.

Even if the copycat denies their copycatting antics, at least they'll know you're onto them.

DON'T GO PUBLIC

While it may be tempting to call the copycatter out on your website or social media, I wouldn't advise it. It may feel good when your fans jump to your defence, but you may quickly become the aggressor instead of the victim.

I once called out a copycat on my Facebook page, taking a screenshot of their thing and comparing it to mine.

At first the comments were supportive. But then it turned nasty, with some people calling him names and calling for blood.

He complained to Facebook and got the post removed, He then started emailing and even calling me, and leaving messages.

In the end, I felt I had to apologise. And even though he admitted to the copycatting, I came off looking like the bad guy.

Slagging off a competitor is never a good look. Take the moral high ground whenever possible.

TAKE LEGAL ACTION

Obviously you should only take this step if:

- You can completely prove the copycatting.
- It's having a serious impact on your business.
- You have oodles of cash – legal stuff is expensive.

Start by consulting a copyright or intellectual property theft lawyer so you know exactly where you stand.

And a simple legal letter can often have a big impact.

But copyright can be very hard prove. The rules vary from country to country, and even from industry to industry. Even if you've trademarked your 'thing', it might not stop someone else from stealing it.

While I'm no legal expert, I consider going down the legal route a serious last resort.

(Note: There's no point getting lawyers involved simply because someone re-shared your meme without a link back to your website.)

EMBRACE YOUR AWESOMENESS

Remember: if you're creating stuff that's worth copying, you've probably got a lot more great ideas stewing in your mind-pot.

Let the copied idea go, and move onto your next project.

THANK YOUR COPYCAT

In business, you always need to stay one step ahead of the competition. You can't get complacent. You need to keep innovating. It's vital to stay close to your customers, understand their needs, solve their problems and keep on delivering awesome 'stuff'.

If you take a grateful approach, then instead of letting copycats get on your nerves you'll be thanking them for keeping you on your toes.

POINTS TO PONDER

If you're struggling with copycats, here are a few simple ways to deal with them:

STOP LOOKING

This is the single most powerful tactic I can recommend. It works for me, and keeps me focused on my own success. Whenever I look at what others are doing I find copycats. Unfortunately, I also tend to throw myself into a pit of self-doubt.

Embracing your competitors is one thing. But if you're embracing them just to look over their shoulder at their computer screen, you need to stop.

SO I RECOMMEND:

- Unsubscribing from your competitors' emails
- Removing yourself from groups where your competitors regularly post (if they irk you)
- Resisting the urge to check out your competitors' websites.

If someone sends you something that mentions copycatting, thank them. But don't look.

WHAT THEY SAY 

Copying is the highest form of flattery. Ignore it, and move on.

WHAT I SAY 

Copying is lazy, selfish and downright mean. It's not flattering. It's exhausting.

Many of us judge ourselves harshly because things like getting copied and worrying about competitors get us down. We look at the well-known entrepreneurs and think, "I bet they never worry about such petty little things."

Believe me, they do.

When you dig deep with other entrepreneurs (generally over a few glasses of wine), they'll openly admit that they sweat the small stuff too. They've just learned to hide it behind a positive veneer. They put on their best face, and never whinge or share stories about the dark days.

Which is yet another reason why I'm a crappy at being an entrepreneur. I prefer honesty. Things like copycats give us all the shits, and learning to deal with it has been a hard journey for me.

But now I can honestly say I'm over it. And you can be too.

CHAPTER 10
FITTING IT ALL IN

I often wish I'd married for money rather than love. But I chose my husband based on his nice arms and his charm – not bank balance.

This means I don't have the luxury of being bankrolled in business. I have to make money.

Also unlike many entrepreneurs I don't have angel investors, partners or super-rich parents.

So I've been squeezing out the money I make on my own. And I've done it not by selling more than anyone else, but by being more profitable than anyone else.

Often I hear business folk complain that:

- They're not making enough money
- They don't have enough time to get everything done

And of course, the two are directly related.

Believe me, I understand how they feel. Life can often feel like nothing more than a race from one household task to another. Sitting down at my desk is the most relaxing part of my day.

But <insert sound of angels singing> this is one area where **I do** fit the entrepreneurial mould!

Yes, I manage to get a lot done. Yes, I'm prolific. Yes, there's a lot of Toon spread around the interweb. And I achieve it all by being super organised.

The interweb is just gushing with advice – unachievable, guilt-inducing advice we all desperately suck up in the hope that we mere mortals can match their level of success. And I've read my fair share of "89 things successful people do before breakfast" and "7 secrets from smug, successful know-it-alls" type posts.

But don't worry. I won't be giving you crazy advice about getting up at 4am to do yoga on the beach. I am, however, going to share how I organise my day.

So if you've ever said to yourself, "If only I could meditate on my private island every day so I can get more email opt-ins", then this chapter is for you.

THE BASICS

Here are some important starter facts about me (in case you don't know):

- **JOB:** Copywriter, SEO Lover, Trainer, Podcaster, Public Speaker
- **HOURS WORKED:** 35-40 pw
- **INCOME:** I'm doing okay
- **WORKING DAYS:** Short days: Monday, Thursday and Friday (school run both ends). Long days: Tuesday and Wednesday (husband does school things). Can also work on Saturday (but try not to)

MY MORNING ROUTINE

I wake up at 4am feeling totally refreshed. After meditating and doing an hour of yoga, I make myself a wholesome green smoothie while listening to whale music.

On alternate days I jog on the beach and swim in the golden morning surf...

Okay, so I'm lying. As much as I'd like to be that person, this is what I'm really like.

I wake up at 7am, often feeling more tired than when I went to bed.

TOONTIP: Conventional advice tells us that early risers are the gods of the business world. But I've tried it, and it sucks. Give me an hour longer lie-in any day. As a parent, I'll take 60 minutes of extra zzzs over pretty much anything. Sleep makes me happy, and a happy me gets more done than a tired, irritable me.

I lurch to the bathroom with a rigid totter, my legs having seized up during the night through extreme lack of exercise.

I have a quick shower and brush my teeth. On a good day I might even brush my hair.

Then I stumble out into the world to either:

- Make breakfast for my small human, prepare backpack/ lunch box, and do the school run
- Walk my dog to the coffee shop for a jumbo three-shot coffee with half a sugar. (Halving the sugar makes me feel healthier.)

GETTING STARTED

There are days when I just want to sod off the entire day and lie in bed bingeing on Netflix while eating crisps. But once I reach my Toon Cave my motivation usually kicks in, helped by the coffee and pumping up Spotify.

I spend the first 30 minutes:

- Clearing out junk mail
- Reviewing real emails (not answering at this stage – just reviewing)
- Making my 'to do' list
- Posting in my Facebook groups
- Acknowledging shares and tags on social media

And I do it all while standing up, having set my Tomato Timer for 25 minutes.

TOONTIP: The Tomato Timer is based on the Pomodoro method, which is a fab way to get stuff done. You work for 25 minutes then take a five-minute break. It's a great way to smash through the first part of your day and get heaps done.

MY 'TO DO' LIST

When it comes to 'to do' lists I'm a pen and paper girl, although I did use Teuxdeux for a while.

Obviously I try to prioritise my list and guess the time needed for each task. But I usually start with a few easy ones to give myself a sense of achievement. Silly I know, but it works.

I have several 'to do' lists running at once. With six websites to maintain and three core lines of business there's a lot to remember.

So I have a 'nice to do' list, as well as a 'must do' list.

TOONTIP: While there are plenty of 'to do' apps out there, for me nothing beats pen and paper. I suggest including a few easy wins at the top of your list ('Go to toilet', 'Turn on computer', 'Find pen', etc.) so you can quickly tick them off and feel like you're winning.

THE FIRST TASK

Mark Twain apparently said:

"Eat a live frog first thing in the morning, and nothing worse will happen to you the rest of the day."

While I'm sure amphibians are an excellent source of protein, I'm guessing this is one of those metaphor thingies. So I recommend, after those first few easy ticks, you start each day by doing the most hideous task first. Get that out of the way and you'll feel all warm and fuzzy inside.

I try to make sure the first proper job I start is a money earner – something I'm being paid for, rather than my own marketing.

Early morning is also when I'm most creative and cognisant, so it's usually when I write client copy.

I try my hardest not to procrastinate, and get stuck in.

PRIORITIES

Although your daily 'to do' list may change, your overall work priorities shouldn't.

My priority list goes something like this:

- Existing client work
- New client luring

- Financial admin – getting paid
- Marketing, self-promotion and blog writing
- Faffing about on social media

It's a simple and effective way to make sure I focus on my customers and don't get sucked into random videos about cats on Facebook. (Well, most of the time.)

CALENDAR

For a while I tried blocking out time for certain things (something I picked up from Darren Rowse at ProBlogger). But it just didn't work for me, and so now my diary is simply for appointments.

I use Google Calendar, and colour-code the appointments based on lines of business.

I try not to have meetings before 10am (in case I do manage to go for that swim) or after 4pm (I'm too pooped). Chats with overseas clients and students (not to mention podcasts) are often after business hours, so I try to limit them to one day a week (Tuesday or Wednesday).

REWARDS

I use social media and fun jobs (I love making and editing videos) as a reward for completing tougher jobs, such as completing the first draft of a client's copydeck.

EXERCISE

I walk my dog to the coffee shop and back every day. I also work to loud music, and have perfected a rather good dance I can do while remaining in my swivelly chair. It's not pretty, but it keeps my bum cheeks pert – vital to being a successful businessperson in my book.

PHONE CALLS

I don't answer my phone. Instead I let the calls go to voicemail, and then call back at a nominated time. This saves me from having to deal with potential tyre kickers, random Indian SEO companies, and friends wanting to come over for a cup of tea. (I love friends and tea, but I'm working.)

SMILE

I once read that when you smile it tricks your brain into thinking you're happy, even when you're not. So if you ever walk past my office window you'll probably see me grinning inanely at the screen. Smiling while you're on the phone also makes you sound much nicer than you possibly are.

MANTRAS

Yep, mantras do work.

You can go with something deep: "The sea otter never asks why the water is wet".

Something inspiring: "Bright stars shine brighter when they love themselves".

Or something practical: "Don't eat the yellow snow".

My favourite mantra is, '"Stop whinging and get on with it". It works every time.

WHAT WORKS WELL

- **Mornings:** I tend to get a lot done in the mornings.
- **Scheduling/batching:** I spend time each month creating and scheduling social media posts all in one go.
- **Project management:** I use Asana to manage all my projects. (I moved to it recently after finding Basecamp a truly painful experience.)

  And I have ready-made projects set up, which means I can 'set and forget' and then wait for the alerts telling me what to do each day. Psst: By 'ready-made projects' I mean templates that are set up with standard tasks for each type of job I do.
- **Documentation:** I have documents for everything. I also have templates for all kinds of project emails, as well as ad hoc things such as interview requests, favour requests and tech issues.
- **Toggl:** I use Toggl to track my time (when I remember to switch it on).
- **Typing:** I type super fast (one of my superpowers).
- **Bravery:** I'm willing to give stuff a go without fear of failure, which means I don't procrastinate much.

WHAT DOESN'T WORK SO WELL

Psst: Check out all the contradictions, which are all part of the entrepreneurial life.

- **Afternoons:** Once it hits 2pm my brain doesn't work so well. I use this fuzzy time to do monotonous tasks such as social media scheduling, WordPress fixes, editing, etc.

- **Scheduling/batching:** I'd also like to batch things like writing blog posts and creating videos. But I tend to do them randomly when the urge takes me, which isn't productive at all.

- **Social media:** It's a huge time suck that I wrestle with all day, every day.

- **Boundaries:** I try to switch off each evening around 3pm (school days) or 6pm (work days). But I often find myself logging in again. (It doesn't help that Netflix is on my laptop, which makes it all too easy to flick over to my work email or business Facebook groups every two seconds.)

- **Bravery:** Because I'm willing to give things a go, I sometimes launch them without thinking things through!

THE HARD TRUTH

Ready for the truth of all this? I work too hard.

Yes, I had many financial successes last year. And I earned almost double what I earned the previous year. But I'm also paying the price:

- I've gained 15 kilos in two years from general lack of exercise and greediness

- I don't make my personal health a priority. At all. Ever

- I get stressed about work, and even get a little manic at times

- I frequently feel overwhelmed, and that I should pack it all in

But on the bright side I spend a lot of quality time with my son, keep a tidy house, and cook the odd meal.

THE WAY FORWARD

I have enough self-awareness to realise that at some point in the past year I was bitten by the entrepreneur bug. And it made me believe I could create a passive income and achieve the four-day working week.

What I did instead was to add two more businesses to my already successful business, and go from working 20 hours a week to working double that.

Yes, I'm financially better for it. But personally? Not so much.

These days my objectives aren't to grow, but rather to maintain the status quo. This will involve:

- Saying 'no' to some opportunities (that often aren't opportunities anyway)
- Holding myself back from fiddling with websites and products
- Stuffing cotton wool in my ears and nose to stop me from coming up with new ideas
- Focusing on what earns me money and what brings me joy!

So there you have it – an insight into my daily working life, my stresses and worries, and my highs and woes.

POINTS TO PONDER

ASK YOURSELF TOUGH QUESTIONS

As a business owner, you must be able to answer these questions:

1. How many hours do you have to work a week?
2. What percentage of your time is actually billable?
3. What is your hourly rate?
4. Based on your billable hours, what are you making each week?

If you're struggling to answer these questions, you have a problem.

Most likely you're in business to make money, and to make money you must keep track of your time.

SET FIRM WORKING HOURS

Make a clear division between your working and non-working time, and stick to it. Yes, we all thought working for ourselves would mean days in coffee shops flicking through magazines. But the truth is, if you want to make money then you need your bum on your office seat for a set number of hours each week.

DECIDE ON AN HOURLY RATE

Set a value on each hour of your time. Lots of online tools can help you work out how much you need to earn based on outgoings, etc. (Of course, you can ignore these and charge what you want.) Divide the weekly amount by your hours and – voila – you have your hourly rate. Or do you?

If you sell products, consider your profit margins, shipping, packaging etc. very carefully. Even digital and virtual products have a cost involved – the cost to create the bloody things in the first place.

TRACK YOUR BILLABLE TIME

Let's be clear: not all working time is billable time. In my experience, very few business owners keep track of their time, perhaps because timesheets remind us of working for 'the man'. But timesheets are your friend. Tools such as Toggl can help you track individual projects and see billable versus non-billable time.

After a few weeks of tracking, I was shocked to discover only 50% of my time was actually earning me money. These days it's a little tougher to track since I don't swap hours for money. But I still try to ensure I'm spending as much time as possible on measurable things.

STOP MARKETING FOR THE HECK OF IT

Yes, it's fun to chat on forums and Facebook groups. But are these people your potential customers? And while you might enjoy writing blogs and creating memes, are you marketing for profit or just for the heck of it?

For example people often ask me how much time they need each week to tackle SEO. My answer is always that they're probably spending enough time already. They're just spending it on the wrong thing.

It's simple – every marketing action needs a goal.

SET UP PROCESSES

Take a day out to look at your business and identify tasks that happen repeatedly. Then set up document templates and email templates, and write up your process from client contact to project completion.

Psst: I have oodles of templates in my store. But I won't mention that here as that would be too salesy.

Not only does this help you manage your clients (and avoid confusion/issues), it also means you'll know what you need to do at each step.

STOP THE CHAT

Answering the phone means having to talk to other humans, and some other humans talk too much. By not answering the phone you can avoid this and get on with your work. I set aside an hour a day to ring people, return messages and deal with phone stuff. After that, I switch it to back silent.

Also try to have any client meetings via Skype or on the phone. If you do have a face-to-face chat, bill your client for the travel time. Limit Skype chats and phone calls to fifteen minutes when you can. Endless client chats is one of the biggest time and profit killers, I know.

Of course, there are heaps of other ways to save time and stop the faff. But the longer I make this chapter the more time you'll spend reading it.

So stop reading now, and go and make some serious moolah.

WHAT THEY SAY 

Organisation is the key to success.

WHAT I SAY 

For once I agree with what 'they' say. Being organised has helped with a lot of things – the frazzled look, the emotions, and the complete lack of plans.

Because I don't have much time, I make the most of the time I have. I don't dilly dally. I don't faff. I just get stuck in.

But I'm also gentle with myself. I can't be a productivity machine every day. I need some downtime.

I don't think there's such a thing as work-life balance. But it is possible to do the things and have a life.

CHAPTER 11

THINGS JUST GOT A LITTLE EMOTIONAL

ENTREPRENEURIAL REQUIREMENT
The even temperament

When I worked in the 'real world' I was passionate and determined about what I did. Elated at my successes and devastated at my mistakes, I rode that business rollercoaster with a white-knuckled grip.

And it didn't go unnoticed.

Not one, but four bosses took me aside and said, "You're great at your job, Kate. But you're way too emotional".

And emotional and entrepreneurial aren't always a good fit.

Emotion is often seen as a strength, especially in men. That bang on desk, 'let's get it done' kind of anger can be powerful and motivating. In fact, over-confidence and bravado are almost a prerequisite.

But I'm talking about crying – snivelly, whingy sobbing. While it's not part of the entrepreneur checklist, it is part of the Toon checklist. And no matter how hard I try to scrub it off, it's still there.

Try as I might to be a calm, centred being, I'm still a very emotional creature. I feel things deeply, as if I have an enlarged and over-productive emotion gland.

My business week isn't exactly a smooth line. I have super high highs and hideous lows. I laugh too loudly, and I'm an ugly crier. I imbue inanimate objects with emotions, and even use the coffee cup at the back of the cupboard so it doesn't feel left out.

I know. I'm starting to sound crazy.

But I proudly stand by my emotions. In fact, I'd go so far as to say being an emotional beast makes me a better entrepreneur.

Why? Because emotion breeds empathy, and empathy helps me understand my customers better.

Being emotional helps me soothe their pain points, and deliver better products and services. I've been there. I get them.

And they, in turn, get me.

Up until about two years ago, I did what every entrepreneur is supposed to do: put a positive spin on everything. I celebrated my successes, shared upbeat stories and turned negatives into positives.

It became a kind of social media grin that I wore every day until my cheeks started aching.

And then I tried being real.

Let's be honest: while it seems fine to harp on about the **practical** challenges of running a business, people tend to clam up about the **mental** and **emotional** ones. We can't admit it's a bloody nightmare sometimes because **that** would destroy the myth of living the entrepreneurial dream.

And we can't have that, can we?

As you've no doubt noticed, I regularly suffer from overwhelm, jealously, FOMO[13] and worthlessness. And yes, it's a bit shit to be honest.

But I found that sharing these stories helped other people. It made

---

[13] Fear Of Missing Out

them feel more normal, more human, and let them know it's okay to enjoy what you do on some days and hate it on others.

Work-related stress is a huge issue in modern day business. And those entrepreneurs selling a fake dream of eternal prosperity are just putting more pressure on the rest of us.

So I think it's important to share the highs **and** the woes. The no-make-up selfies, the messy desks, and the piles of washing next to the laptop.

As business people, we need to admit that we're not exercising enough. That we only shampoo our fringes for Skype calls. And that we often feel guilty about spending too much time working and not enough time living.

Being an openly emotional entrepreneur might not quite fit the mould. But it helped me connect with thousands of people in a way I could only have imagined if my photos were of me looking tanned and fabulous in my perfect home, with my Instagrammable breakfast.

I'm not saying you should share your every waking thought on social media. And you should temper the sad and bad stories with good and uplifting ones. The last thing you want is to your turn your business feed into a whinge fest.

What I **am** saying is that it's often helpful to show your human side. To share your stories – good **and** bad. And to talk about the mistakes you've made, and what you learned from them.

A buddy of mine who's a well-known female entrepreneur recently burst into tears at a conference we were attending. I won't go into the reasons why, but suffice to say she was a little bit embarrassed.

Until she wasn't.

Instead of beating herself up, she turned the incident into a lesson. She examined why it happened, took a good hard look at herself, and turned it into a story she could share with her business colleagues.

The result? She took a weepy, emotional moment and turned it into a positive for both herself and her business. It also made me love her that little bit more: vulnerability is a hugely attractive quality in my eyes.

POINTS TO PONDER

If you're an emotional beast like me, here are some ways you can use that emotion for business good, instead of feeling crap about it.

SHARE A STORY

The next time you have a run-in with a client, or send an email to your mailing list with a typo in the first line, try sharing it with your readers. My guess is you'll be overwhelmed with 'me too' comments.

HELP OTHERS

Even if you're only a week into your business journey, you're already a week ahead of anyone who hasn't started out yet. And that means they can learn from you. So take the time to offer help in forums and groups. It may not always be warmly received, but chances are you will help some of your audience. And it will make you feel good too.

BE AWARE

I'm a great believer in pushing on through. But I also know when I've had enough, or when I'm just feeling a bit down and know it's not a good time to tackle the big thing.

Being someone who has their ups and downs is actually a good thing. When we're up we can achieve great things. But only if we take note of our down times and don't beat ourselves up about them.

WHAT THEY SAY 

As an entrepreneur, confidence and emotional resilience are key.

WHAT I SAY 

While part of me would love to be an emotionless automaton, I know that my slightly over-sensitive, jealous, angry, weepy self is utterly adorable.

Okay, I jest. A little. I **would** like to be less emotional. But I'm pretty much halfway through my life, and I think my emotions are part of who I am. Being emotionally sensitive, and feeling things so keenly has its pros and cons. And accepting who I am is much easier and nicerer than disliking myself every day.

CHAPTER 12

OOH, LOOK, SPARKLY THING

ENTREPRENEURIAL REQUIREMENT

A single-minded vision

Any good 'How to be an entrepreneur' book will tell you that taking risks is a great thing. And any self-respecting entrepreneur's biography will include a story about how they took an idea everyone else thought would fail and turned it into something awesome.

But how do you know if your shiny thing is *the* shiny thing?

The truth is, along with not having a plan I'm a huge fan of rashly rushing into projects and submitting to 'shiny new object' syndrome.

I don't do A/B testing (check the glossary if you're not sure what this is), run surveys or create a beta version for anything I do. I just go live with it – pretty much immediately.

The 'better done than perfect and undone' mantra is something I live by.

Admittedly it has led to some horrendous last-minute panics and horribly late nights. But it also means my products and services are out there, in all their imperfect glory, earning me money.

Of course, it helps that I'm happy to admit my failures rather than clinging to my mistakes just because they took so long to make.

We're always being told that going after the shiny thing is bad, and that we should plan, consider and think things through instead.

Well, I'm here to tell you it isn't true.

INNOVATE THEN ITERATE

I have **never** waited until something was complete before it went live. Sometimes I get so excited about blog posts that I publish them while I'm still adding graphics.

A perfect case in point is my SEO ecourse.

After creating a rough outline I wrote a sales page and made it live. I ended up selling 20 or so spaces in the first round.

Then I worked out how to actually make an ecourse. I frantically worked out the subject matter, made videos, created worksheets, and set up Facebook groups. And thanks to my crappy internet connection, sometimes the week's lesson would finish uploading seconds before it was due to go live.

It was stressful and hideous and glorious.

And it made perfect business sense. Imagine if I built the whole course and sold only one ticket. Even a test webinar or micro course wouldn't have proven the full course would sell.

My random, crazy approach worked perfectly. I had the money in the bank before I took the risk, so it wasn't really a risk at all.

But the important factor behind it all is the willingness to start again.

Obviously the first round of my course while great, wasn't perfect. And since then I've revamped the course materials twice because I'm willing to learn from my mistakes and start again.

Yes, I'm happy with 'done' rather than 'perfect'. But that doesn't mean I won't keep trying to perfect it after it's done.

ACCEPTING MY LIMITATIONS

I spent a long time accepting my limitations, a few of which I've covered in this book. But it wasn't until I started ignoring them completely that I really ramped up my business.

I've already talked about how my fear of not looking right stopped me making videos and doing any public speaking. Well, when I let go of that fear and started booking speaking jobs, it transformed my business. It gave me more authority, more confidence, and helped spread my name farther and wider.

I wasn't a trained **SEO** consultant either, and so felt I couldn't pass what I knew on to others. But when I let that go I found people were happy to learn from me. I didn't need to teach the uber-advanced subjects. Instead I could help people truly grasp the foundations.

By grabbing that shiny thing by the wiggly bits, I created a whole new line of business that now generates around 70% of my overall revenue.

And letting go of the idea that people wouldn't pay for my advice and coaching allowed me to start my own membership group for copywriters. And that led to me setting up Australia's first dedicated copywriting conference for those members.

I understand my limitations now. But I don't let them limit me.

JUST BECAUSE I CAN DOESN'T MEAN I SHOULD

As I mentioned at the beginning of this book, I don't have a string of failed businesses behind me. I've started three, and they've all been successful. They've made money, helped people, and made me happy.

Which sometimes makes me think I could create **more** businesses that would be just as successful.

I get a lot of ideas. But lucky for me (and my husband) I remember that just because I could doesn't mean I should.

Right now I'm happy with the businesses I have. But it doesn't stop me from having mini daft ideas and tangents. One time I thought about selling **SEO** tea towels, and I'm sure I would have sold a few. But what would have been the point?

Another time I started randomly offering illustrations to people on Facebook. It was fun, but once again pointless.

On a larger scale, I set up an entire subcontracting arm to my *Clever Copywriting School,* then quickly trashed it when I remembered how much I hated project management.

These days, I judge every opportunity by four questions:

- Does it support one of my three businesses?
- Will I enjoy doing it?
- Will it make me money?
- Is it something my customers want?

Three yeses makes it a 'maybe'. And four usually makes it a sure thing.

I'm a huge fan of Sparkly Thing Syndrome. It leads to discoveries and improvements, and keeps me excited about my business. And while I wouldn't call myself a risk taker, I'm not afraid to fall on my face either.

No one wants to look like a fool. But a little controlled foolery is just fine.

POINTS TO PONDER

Do you suffer from Sparkly Thing Syndrome? Here's some advice on how to tackle it:

ARE YOU BORED, OR ACTUALLY BURNED OUT?

I'm often attracted to new projects when I'm a bit fed up with what I'm currently working on. It's worth taking a step back and having a break from the day-to-day so you can revisit the sparkly thing with a fresh mind.

HOW MUCH OF A COMMITMENT WILL YOU HAVE TO MAKE?

If the sparkly thing involves little financial investment and a fraction of your time, it may well be worth the risk. Even if your side project or experiment flops, it could add a new dimension to your overall business.

At the very least, you'll be able to cross another item off your business bucket list.

WHAT THEY SAY 

Focus. Focus. Focus.

WHAT I SAY 

What a dull world it would be if we did everything we were supposed to, slavishly ticking off items on our to do list without so much as a glance at Netflix.

For me, the best parts of my journey have been the diversions – the side streets, dead ends and roundabouts. A lot of the sparkly things people mocked early on have become my core business offering. And as a bonus I now have enough tea towels to last a lifetime.

CHAPTER 13
TWO'S COMPANY

One question I've struggled with a lot over the years is whether I need a team to be successful.

And again, by 'successful' I mean earning enough money to get by and having enough time to do what I want in both my business and my life.

I'm still not sure I have an answer.

One very successful entrepreneur I spoke to at a recent event told me in no uncertain terms that I'll never grow my business the way I want to on my own.

There are only so many hours in the day, and only so much of me to go around. And I'm better off spending that time creating new 'things' rather than reconciling Xero payments – no matter how brainless and enjoyable it can be at the end of a long day.

But also I know I don't play well with others. Remember that enlarged and over-productive emotion gland I mentioned in chapter 11? Well, it's a problem. I'm a sensitive sausage, and that can be painful when working with a team.

Oh, and I have very little patience for people who don't 'get' things quickly – even if I've done a terrible job explaining it to them.

Add to that the fact I generally think my way is the best way, and you can see what a giant pain in the arse I am.

Part of my reason for leaving the corporate world was that I didn't want to have a boss. But the other part is that I was such a terrible boss myself.

So it's hard for me to employ other people, even if they're doing work for me from the other side of the world.

For a long time I had a small team of these virtual helpers.

As the hours grew so did their numbers. And it wasn't long before I was stressing about having to assign and check their work on top of doing my own.

But then my wonderful Virtual Assistant (VA) told me she'd found a full-time job. And as I congratulated her I had to choke back tears of sadness and panic.

And it got worse. My other Virtual Assistant (yes, I had two) also got a full-time job. My designer then announced she was off on an extended holiday. And did I mention my cleaner resigned?

All of a sudden, my Downton Abbey-esque team of helpers was down to a skeleton staff.

And I was completely reliant on these people. It's been ages since I've coded a blog post or tweeted a tweet.

I panicked.

And then I stopped, took a breath, and did that thing we're supposed to do: turn a negative into a positive.

Having decided to turn it into a learning experience, I went without help for two months and used the time to evaluate whether having a team was working for me.

I took on less. I did less. And I was a **lot** less stressed.

You see, a huge part of me hated having a team. Yes, I was earning more money. But I was also working harder than I'd ever planned (or even imagined), because no matter how autonomous my helpers were they needed to be managed.

And I was spending all of my time monitoring and checking other people's work instead of doing what I love the most: creating.

It was the same at home, where I'd amassed a hoard of helpers: cleaner, gardener, babysitter, handyman and occasional dog walker. It was only a matter of time before I hired someone to eat for me, sleep for me and wipe my bum.

It began to feel like I'd outsourced my entire life. And you know what? It was bloody exhausting.

I started my business so I could be in control. But as your business grows it can turn into a bit of a beast, and pretty soon it's controlling you.

Unfortunately, not having a team left me feeling frustrated. I couldn't get through my tasks, and it was taking too long to get my business where I wanted it to be.

So I slowly started building up my team again.

I tried the overseas VA thing three times, but it never worked for me. Language was never an issue, but their sense of humour (or lack of it) often was. And I never felt any understanding, camaraderie, or even confidence that they cared about the work they were doing as much as their hourly wage.

Since then I've gone back to having an Australian VA (shout out to Leanne). I hired:

- A part-time bookkeeper – an easy win (thanks Alec)
- A regular coder (thanks Marco)
- A fabulous part-time designer (hugs to Kate)

I've also outsourced some of my event management, PR and email set up. It's a bit of a mashup, but so far so good.

And here's what I've learned along the way.

1. GIVE MORE TIME

Even the best Virtual Assistant is only as good as your briefing.

I now use Asana to outline my tasks, and try to make them as detailed as possible – a far cry from what they used to be like: "Can you add that thing to the site where the other thing we did was last week?"

My VA is pretty good at interpreting my Toonspeak. But as you can imagine even she gets lost sometimes.

Of course, in the time it takes to explain what needs doing I could probably do it myself. But you have to play the long game. And you need to invest in them without being scared that they'll leave you for another, more sexy entrepreneur.

TOONTIP: You need to invest some serious time in training your team before you can leave them to it. But once they've got it, the investment will soon pay off.

2. TAKE YOUR TIME

As I mentioned in the sparkly thing chapter, I always have some new scheme in development – a fresh idea, or a sparkly plan. And having a team of helpers means I can put these into action very quickly.

Knowing I have retainer hours to fill each month, I'll often start them working on a project before I've completely thought it through. And then as time goes on it needs more and more tweaks to get it right – all of which I'm paying for.

TOONTIP: Just because you can do it straight away doesn't mean you should do it straight away. Slow down and plan.

3. HAVING A TEAM CAN MEAN MORE WORK

The people in my virtual team are super autonomous. But they're not me.

It's my name on those 197 business cards, and every fluff up needs to be owned by yours truly. (I don't play the blame game.) This means I have to double-check every piece of work, which eats up a huge amount of time.

And if you have a team member who works for you at a set time each week, you need to be available whenever they have a question or it will be another week before you can fix it.

TOONTIP: Just because you have help doesn't mean you can let go completely.

4. HAVING A TEAM IS EXPENSIVE

Having a virtual team costs money. Obvious, right? But it took me a while to understand that every cent I spent on outsourcing was an extra cent I had to earn.

According to my accountant I had a good year last year. But when I look at my balance sheet, all I see is that I spent more money on my team than I earned in my first year of business.

And that makes me uncomfy.

I set up my own business because I never wanted to have staff. I never wanted to be responsible for paying someone else's mortgage. But having staff on retainers means my wage is paying their wage. And it took me a long time to get used to that kind of pressure.

The more comfortable I became with my business, the more confident I become in what I'm doing. And the more willing I am to invest in it – and in good people.

TOONTIP: It's important to understand the ROI on getting help, and be clear about whether it will truly improve your profitability.

POINTS TO PONDER

If you're thinking about growing your team, here are a few suggestions that might help:

WHAT CAN YOU OUTSOURCE?

One mistake a lot of business owners make is clinging onto the bits of the business they like best, or the bits they find hardest to let go of.

It's a mistake to think your team can only help you with the easy or monotonous tasks. Get them involved in higher-level tasks to keep them engaged and free yourself up more.

TAKE TIME TO TRAIN

I made screencasts of most of my tasks and uploaded them to Vimeo for my assistants. I also invested in some proper task management software to make it easier to track them. (The tasks, not my assistants.)

Finally, I created a handbook for my business – a bible of sorts – and gave my assistants an hour each week to write up what they learned in the handbook. So if they'd worked on something new, I asked them to articulate the steps they'd taken.

Then I checked, corrected and added more detail.

INVEST FULLY

Investing a few hours here and there in a VA or other assistant will make very little difference to your business. It wasn't until I started paying for around ten hours a week that I saw a real difference. Ten hours is enough time for the VA to get stuck into tasks and take ownership

---

WHAT THEY SAY 

You'll never grow your business without a team.

WHAT I SAY 

The truth is that working solo is a lonely business. While I was less stressed working alone, I was also less positive. There was no-one to bounce ideas off, share highs and lows with, or tell me when to pull my head in.

My team is now an important part of my business, not only for what they do but also for who they are as people. They provide me with invaluable advice, camaraderie, support and giggles.

Investing in a team is a risk. The more you give, the more indispensable they become. For a while that fear held me back from working with good people, but now it's a risk I'm willing to take.

I may not have a giant team of millennials squatting on beanbags in a trendy warehouse. But my virtual team of co-workers works just fine for me.

CHAPTER 14
CAN I HAVE THIS DANCE?

As I said earlier, I don't play well with others. I never have.

While I can manage to be a sociable human for a while, it isn't long before I want to scurry back into my hole and hide.

Many entrepreneurs will tell you there's strength in numbers, and in partnering with others to propel you both towards greater success.

But it's something I struggle with.

In my experience, partnerships are rarely equal relationships. In business, as in love, there's always the one who kisses and the one who offers the cheek.

At least, that's how it had always been for me. The division of effort was never equal. I either felt bad because I wasn't doing enough, or hard done by because I was doing so much.

And then there's the whole friend thing. Working with a stranger is tough because you don't know them, their foibles, their strengths or their weaknesses. But working with a friend means you're always in danger of ruining the relationship.

Early on in my business I decided not to work for friends. There would be no mate's rates, and no contras[14]. When any of my friends needed work done I'd refer them to a good person in my network. It was easier and cleaner.

But as time went on, I was offered more and more opportunities to partner with other entrepreneurs. And I approached these 'opportunities' with the utmost caution.

THE HOT COPY PODCAST

The first major partnership was with my podcasting co-host, Belinda Weaver.

I'd briefly mentioned doing a podcast because I got a new microphone. I had no idea what was involved. It was simply my latest shiny thing, and may never have happened. But when Belinda saw the post on social media she suggested we join forces, and the Hot Copy podcast was born.

I'd be lying if I said it's all been smooth sailing. Belinda and I didn't know each other that well, and in the early days we had a fair few miscommunications.

I still feel guilty that she does more, and often forget to do my share of things.

When we first started I thought the podcast was taking up way too much time. But I stuck with it because I didn't want to let Belinda down.

And I'm so glad I did. It's now one of my favourite business bits, and one of the most powerful ways to build my business brands. These days I genuinely look forward to our chats, even if I do always arrive late and slightly grumpy. (Sorry, B.)

---

[14] Contras are where you swap work of a similar nature with another business. So example, I'll write your copy if you build my website. They really suck because the expectations of what is equal to what vary so much.

Belinda and I don't have a formal contract. But then again all we've really invested in the podcast is our time. And knowing her as well as I do now, I'm sure that if there's another miscommunication, or one of us wants out, we'll both handle it gracefully.

It's been a huge partnership win.

WRITE FOR BUSINESS

The second adventure I partnered up for was with Jesse Forrest. And again, he came to me.

Jesse had been offered a presenter role on Dale Beaumont's Brin app, presenting a show on copywriting. And Jesse asked me to be his co-host.

I still don't understand why. I'd met Jesse once, got quite squiffy (a bit drunk) and repeatedly told him he sounded South African. (He's Australian.) And when I say 'repeatedly' I mean I went on and on about it.

I was a buffoon.

But he asked me anyway, and I said yes.

The show we created took hours and hours of work. It was exhausting (five episodes in one day), nerve wracking (neither of us had any TV presentation training), but also hilariously funny.

Jesse may look normal, but he's a hilarious human. We had a lot of giggles.

We planned to do a lot more together after the show, but contractual issues made it hard. Well, that and the fact Jesse decided to move to Thailand and become a digital nomad. The git.

I've yet to see whether doing the show will have any positive impact on my business. But it was a great experience, and another partnership win.

Of course, I could also share some stories of partnerships that didn't work out.

Partnerships where the other person didn't do that thing, where I didn't do that thing, where expectations weren't met, or where we simply danced around each other for a while before deciding it wasn't a good idea.

POINTS TO PONDER

Are you thinking about joining forces with another business person? Here are some considerations for you to... well, consider.

DO YOU LIKE THEM?

Enjoying the person's company is an important first step. I think sharing a similar outlook and sense of humour is hugely important. Your personalities can be different, but you must be able to work well together and communicate.

WHAT'S AT STAKE?

Is the person a life-long friend? What would happen if it all went tits up? Consider whether the risk of it failing is worth the risk of it succeeding. I like to keep friends and business buddies on different shelves of my life fridge.

GET IT IN WRITING

There have been a few times where I didn't spend time writing down what the partnership involved. And yes, they were a disaster.

Although it can be painful, it's important to write down what you and your partner need and expect from the relationship – exit strategies, financial commitments, and whatever else you can think of.

WHAT THEY SAY 

The power of two beats the power of one.

WHAT I SAY 

Joining forces with another person is nerve-racking, and definitely out of my comfort zone.

But when it works, the benefits are huge. The power of two is more than the sum of its parts.

Belinda and I have noticed that the other's success contributes to our own. We have each other's back, and we share each other's followers. And even though she's essentially my competitor, we actually help each other hugely.

So, while I know a partnership can be a fast track to success, it's still something I consider very carefully. And I think you should too.

CHAPTER 15
THE REAL JOB WOBBLES

You love your job, right? You love your small business every minute of every day.

And you share that enthusiasm relentlessly through a stream of happy selfies, inspirational memes and positive thoughts.

Because there are never days when it all seems too hard. And you never think about packing it all in.

My guess is we all have the wobbles from time to time.

As my business has grown, and I've gone from barely having enough money to buy dog food to earning a regular income. But, even so, I seem to be worrying more and more.

Because some days I just can't be arsed with it all.

I'm not sure whether it's:

- The constant need to squeeze out the dollars
- The relentless pressure of competition
- The grating irritation of copycat businesses
- The arse-clenching struggle to motivate myself through each day.

As the clock strikes midnight and you're struggling to stay awake, you begin to question everything you're doing as you fall down the self-doubt rabbit hole:

- "Why am I doing the thing?"
- "Is my thing the right thing?"
- "Do people even want my thing?"
- "Am I the right person to be giving them the thing?"

And after a few hours down this business burrow you start questioning your abilities, your personality and even your personal hygiene.

We've all had moments like these. Moments when things get so bad you dust off our CV, start scrolling through real jobs, and ponder whether you really would be better off working for 'the man'. Sometimes it becomes more than a fleeting thought, and you miss having a real job the way you'd miss a limb.

Now I know some of you will be hissing "Traitor!" through clenched teeth. But before you start hurling mousemats at me and driving me from the solo village with sharpened biros, hear me out.

These are just some of the things I miss about having a real job:

PERFORMANCE REVIEWS

While some people's bum cheeks clench at the mere thought of an annual review, I loved them. I guess there's still a little Kate Toon from high school in me who needs to know how she's doing from time to time.

But now I have to pat my own back. And with my short, T-Rex-like arms, that ain't easy.

THE STATIONERY CUPBOARD

Remember when highlighters and Post-it notes were 'free'? When you could get all the staples you could… er, staple from the glorious stationery cupboard? When you could use one page of a notepad then carelessly toss it aside because you weren't paying for the next one?

Now I use pens to the last blot of ink, and write on both sides of the paper. The environment may be happier, but I'm not.

BUYING LUNCH

I still remember those happy days when I could pop out for sushi, nip out for some Italian, or grab some noodles on the go. The culinary universe was just a hop, skip and jump away from my cubicle.

Now my lunch options include leftovers, toast and cereal because I'm too disorganised to buy enough nice food to sustain me through the week.

FLIRTING

Who doesn't love a harmless work flirt? Coquettish remarks about paper jams. Giggles over who used your coffee mug. Downloading viruses just so the cute IT dude would come and tell you to turn your PC off and on again.

Now my flirting options include my dog, my husband (who also works at home) and my decrepit postman – none of which I find particularly appealing.

GETTING PAID FOR DOING NOTHING

(Note to previous bosses: Please skip this section.)

When I had a real job, I spent a lot of my time trying to do as little as possible. I gave myself countless mini breaks with endless trips to the kitchen, the loo and the coffee shop just to relieve the monotony.

These mini breaks probably added up to a few hours each week. But it didn't matter because I still got paid for them. And at 6pm I'd merrily head home to have a life.

When you're your own boss, there's a temptation to work every nanosecond of the day. And for a long time I did this. I'd start early in the morning and work late into the night, trying to squeeze every possible drop of work juice out of the day.

As the meme goes, "Working for yourself gives you the freedom to work whichever 70 hours a week you like".

But then I realised it totally defeated the point of being my own boss. Here I was sweating that it was nearly school pick up time, when in actual fact one of the reasons I'd started my own business was so I could be there at school pick up time.

So I've pulled right back, and work a lot lesserer hours. But I still miss the simplicity of the real joy work routine sometimes.

THE MONEY

Ah, regular wages. Remember them? The freedom to set up direct debits with abandon because you knew the money would always be there.

And let's not forget paid leave, sick days, expense accounts, cab charges...

It all seems such a distant memory now.

PERSONAL APPEARANCE

Believe it or not I used to buy work outfits. I'd actually coordinate my top and my trousers. I even used to wear shoes.

Now I'm lucky if I change my PJs more than once a week.

I once cared about personal maintenance. I wore make-up, brushed my hair, and plucked my eyebrows. Not anymore, which is why my eyebrows now meet in the middle of my back.

FRIDAY NIGHT DRINKS

Fridays used to mean something. Getting to Friday felt like an achievement, and because I worked in agency land it also meant free booze (and lots of it). A glass of wine would appear on my desk around 4pm, and by 5pm I'd be dancing on the pool table.

It doesn't mean anywhere near as much when your drinking companion is a dog and you have to work on Saturday morning.

On the plus side, my liver is happier.

There are plenty more things I could talk about: the birthday cakes, the IT support, the free business trips, and so on.

But maybe I'm remembering it all with rose-tinted glasses. After all, I also had to put up with hideous commutes, unpaid overtime, office politics, terrible bosses, and the relentless tedium of being a wage slave.

It's easy to fantasise about the steady wage, annual leave and sick days, and being able to completely switch off after work. But to be honest I could never go back to having a 'real' job. For one, I doubt anyone would take me on – especially now that I've admitted to having all those mini breaks.

So my CV is now back in its trusty old folder. My job recruitment website searches are a secret between me and my browser. And I'm back to feeling confident that having a proper job just wouldn't work out for me.

My business is where my heart truly lies. And so I'm just going to do my best, and hope it's good enough.

POINTS TO PONDER

KEEP ON KEEPING ON

One way to deal with the wobbles is to totally ignore them. Stop overthinking things, and just hunker down and do the work.

- Send out those proposals
- Tweet those tweets
- Call those clients
- And put one meme in front of another

WE ALL HAVE BAD DAYS

You can't be 'rah rah rah' all the time, nor do you need to be. It's okay to put down the pom poms every so often and admit that running a business of any size is a tough gig. After all, if it were easy then everyone would be doing it, right?

WHAT THEY SAY 

If you love what you do, you'll never work a day in your life.

WHAT I SAY 

What a crock of poo! We all hate our jobs at one point or another. Even when we work for ourselves it's not all rainbows and unicorns. There are days when my boss (that's me) drives me up the wall, I get sick of the internet, I hate my office, and I just want to run for the hills.

Just because we've found our dream job doesn't mean it isn't a total nightmare sometimes.

CHAPTER 16
THE BELLY FLOP

At some point while running your business, things will go to shit.

Every entrepreneur has a tale of when things went south, and how they turned adversity into prosperity. But what we don't hear about are all the businesses that fail. And most businesses do fail in the first year.

Some days it's hard enough finding your business mojo and scraping together enough enthusiasm just to get through the day. But when things really go wrong, it's easy to start dreaming of the warm comfort and stupefying tedium of working for 'the man'.

And then something good happens, and you're high as a kite again. A cool new project plops into your inbox, an interesting opportunity knocks at your door, or a customer writes you a glowing testimonial.

The truth is that running a small business is a constant series of peaks and troughs, feasts and famines. Your business crumpet lands butter side down one day, and butter side up the next.

So how do you deal with this business rollercoaster?

SEEK SUPPORT

When you're having a bad day, or even a bad month, having a network of shoulders to cry on and ears to bend really helps. You can often find resolution simply by talking it out even in an online forum.

The people you choose to whinge to don't have to be friends or family. (In fact, they're often the worst choices).

Instead, try an online forum or group. (I have a few that you're more than welcome to join.)

FOCUS ON THE POSITIVE

I know it's easier said than done. But when things are going wrong try to think of one thing, however small, that went right.

I tried doing the jar of positive mantra things, but I ended up dumping the mantras and filling it with sherbet lemons instead.

BE REALISTIC

While it's important to have plans, it's equally important not to get too attached to them. Yes, you wanted to achieve X by Y. But does the fact you haven't really matter?

Don't stress if your ebook is a month late (like this one), or you miss posting a blog or two. Most of your customers won't even realise. And those who do realise won't actually give a crap.

Although it often feels **ALL ABOUT YOU**, in my experience it rarely is.

FIND PERSPECTIVE

Try to remember that you're not curing cancer (unless you actually are an oncologist). So what if your computer explodes and you miss a deadline? Big deal. While your client may be disappointed, or even angry, it's not the end of the world.

AVOID NEGATIVITY

Stay away from the poo-pooers and negative thinkers who fill your head with doom and gloom. And avoid those who let you wallow in self-pity for too long.

Don't get me wrong. I love a good wallow. But sometimes you need more of a slap in the face than a gentle hug of reassurance. Try to cultivate a bunch of people who will be fair, but firm, with you.

DO WHAT YOU LOVE

If you truly love what you do, you'll cling to that rollercoaster for dear life. Think of your business like your annoying toddler who's just spilt juice on the couch for the fifth time. It may well be annoying, and even costly. But you still love them to bits, and wouldn't trade them for anything.

TAKE A BREAK

When everything looks bleak it's sometimes worth stepping away from your business for a while, whether it's a one-hour yoga session or a sneaky day off at the movies dripping bits of choc top on your t-shirt.

Spending some time away from your business can often help you see things more clearly. And even if you don't get any perspective, at least you've been able to catch the latest Tom Hardy flick.

BUILD PROCESSES

Some businesses face the same problem again and again. If yours is one of them, try to learn from the experience, and create a process or plan to handle it the next time it happens.

I spent ages writing the same emails to all my clients. So after a while I created a template for each one, with gaps for personalisation, and saved them onto my desktop for easy access.

Later I turned this template into a product in my Clever Copywriting Shop for other copywriters, and now not only do they help me be more efficient, they also earn me some cashola.

BE KIND TO YOURSELF

There's no doubt that running a business is hard and often a bit sucky.

I'm sure you'd agree that building and managing your own enterprise takes guts, determination, hard work and intelligence. But you also need compassion - not just for your clients, but also for yourself.

I am not a nice boss. I constantly criticise myself, expect too much, and rarely give myself a day off. So once in a while I have to have a good hard word with myself. I have to push back and threaten to resign.

Remember to give yourself a pat on the back once in a while, and be proud of everything you've achieved so far.

WHAT THEY SAY 

Failure is not an option.

WHAT I SAY 

While it might not be an option, it is an inevitability. So you'd better learn to deal with it.

Remember why you started your business in the first place, and use it as a light to guide you through the dark times.

Running your own business can be emotional and stressful. But never forget that working for someone else has its own stresses.

You may be a rollercoaster, but at least you get to choose your own seat. So hang on tight, get through the lows, and enjoy the highs.

CHAPTER 17
YOU'RE A SUCCESS! WHAT NEXT?

ENTREPRENEURIAL REQUIREMENT

Ongoing success

There came a time a few years ago when I realised my businesses were going swimmingly:

I had quality enquiries coming in every day:

- My cashflow was steady, and my income and profits were increasing nicely each year
- My customers were happy and returning for more
- My courses were selling
- My follower numbers were increasing

Everything was tickety-boo.

I'd overcome the challenges of creating a niche in a crowded market. I'd managed to balance the whole mum/work thing. I'd been through some serious business storms and weathered them well. In fact, I'd made pretty much every mistake in the book and learned from them all.

I should have been patting myself on the back for a job well done. I should have been happy.

But I wasn't.

You see, smooth sailing is just that – smooth. And while smooth can be comforting, or even easy, it's rarely exciting or interesting.

I'd fallen into the dreaded business rut.

I kept thinking, "What next?" and drawing a blank. How could I keep my business fresh? And where could I find the motivation to keep going?

Actually, I started feeling like this last year, which led to a little bit of self-sabotage. Drunk on success, I threw caution out of the window and started making **really** crazy decisions.

I started burning through cash.

"I've got money in the bank, so why don't I randomly build myself a crazily expensive cubby house in the back garden and spend thousands on kitting it out. Oh, and I may as well replace my perfectly fine Mac while I'm at it."

I also started procrastinating wildly. There were so many things I **could** do that I became overwhelmed and ended up doing nothing.

Even as I'm writing this book I'm juggling a heap of other super important projects.

So how did I get through this? Well, I tried a few important things.

TALKING TO PEOPLE

Getting a fresh perspective on your business can be tough sometimes. That's why it's often a good to talk to someone else (other than your partner and your dog).

I'm too cheap to pay for a coach or join someone else's mastermind. So I started my own, and invited some like-minded creatures at a similar stage in their business to join.

Being able to get their perspective on things was incredibly helpful.

LEARN DETACHMENT

When you're starting a business, you often need to give it your all. Pretty soon it takes over your life and becomes all-consuming.

So now that your business is working fine, isn't it time for a little separation?

I've struggled with how my job has become a major part of my identity. I am my business, which makes it almost impossible to switch off.

Having a level of detachment between me and my business helps me gain perspective, and see new opportunities more easily.

REMEMBER THE LOVE

While it's easy for me to focus on the technical side of my business (the accounts, the marketing, and all that jazz), it can be good sometimes to go back to basics and remember why I love what I do.

Whether you're a tiler, a hairdresser, a web developer or a copywriter, one of the best ways to stay engaged and interested is to focus on the actual bread and butter of your job.

Sometimes the only way to fight the lethargy is to just get stuck in and get stuff done.

ENJOY A 'FALLOW PERIOD'

If you're feeling a little burned out, taking a break can help recharge your wiggly bits. You don't necessarily need to head off on holiday. You can simply take your foot off the accelerator and cruise for a while.

I call this my 'fallow period'. It's a farming term that means letting the field lie unplanted for a year so the nutrients can return to the soil. Who knows what could grow next year?

So don't be afraid to just do your work for a while without constantly thinking about the next big thing.

FIND DIRECTION

If you feel a little rejuvenated at the end of your fallow period, perhaps it's time to work out a new direction.

Last year I set myself some business challenges to move me out of my comfort zone and breathe new life into my business. And they definitely put some pep into my step.

Pivot. Change. Shake things up. Push them further. How could this business possibly be profitable without you?

UNDERSTAND YOUR VERSION OF SUCCESS

Sometimes we're so busy looking for the next bright shiny object that we forget how far we've come and what we've achieved.

Think about what you've achieved so far, and write down the highlights. You'll not only feel all warm and gooey in your happy crevices, but also feel more positive about the future.

REDEFINE FUTURE SUCCESS

Our vision of success changes over the year as our goals shift. We may have been happy to simply stay afloat or earn a lot of money, but now we need something more.

LOOK OUTSIDE OF YOUR BUSINESS

Remember when you started out, and hoped running your own business would give you the chance to do new things? Not work-related things, but real life things – learning to play piano, mastering karate, or taking long walks on the beach.

Well, now's the time.

There's nothing wrong with changing your perspective on your business. You're allowed to think of it as a relatively enjoyable way to earn some money. You don't need to be conquering your business Mount Everest all the time.

KNOW WHEN TO KEEP ON KEEPING ON

Sometimes it feels like your business has run out of gas, and you crave something new. Trouble is, you might not know what that 'something new' actually is.

My advice? Just keep on keeping on until something new appears that tickles your fancy.

KNOW WHEN TO THROW IN THE TOWEL

There comes a time in every business owner's life when enough is enough. There's no more fuel in your business tank, and you feel it's time to try something different.

But how do you know if that time is now? Try not to make rash decisions. If you are going to throw in the towel don't hurl it on the bathroom floor like an angry teenager. Instead take time to consider your options, weigh up the pros and cons – fold that towel gently and carefully before you throw it away.

TAKE RESPONSIBILITY

The joy and agony of running a small business is that it's all on you. It's important to realise that only you have the power to keep your business mojo going. You're the only person who can make you happy doing what you're doing. And that means you have to make an effort to be positive.

WHAT THEY SAY 

Success feels great.

WHAT I SAY 

Success feels odd. And it can also be a slippery little sucker. Just when you think you've made it, the finish line moves further away. When you think you've reached your peak, you see your competitor waving from an even higher peak.

And when you've put all your emotional eggs into one omelette, that omelette often doesn't taste as good as you'd hoped.

If goals are your thing, I recommend having some real life goals as well as business goals.

Who would have thought having a successful business wasn't enough?

CHAPTER 18
GO BIG OR GO HOME

A well-known entrepreneur type recently contacted me and offered to help 'up-level' my business in return for a bit of public back scratching.

He was keen to take my six-figure business and add a zero.

And my response was, "Why would I want that?"

While I get the whole money thing, the truth is I'm quite comfy at the moment. There's nothing I particularly want, and certainly nothing I need. In fact, I've reached the stage where I'm replacing perfectly good cushions with newer perfectly good cushions.

I don't need any more cushions.

And yet people still insist that 'big is beautiful', and that the only path to success is continual growth. You have to keep shimmying up the business pole or you'll start slipping down again. You should be aiming high, expanding your network, making a name for yourself, and getting your brand out there.

But what's wrong with staying small? What if every time you ask yourself whether it's time to scale up your business your inner voice shouts "No!" at the top of its lungs?

Are you a victim of 'small thinking', or simply content with what you've got?

Believe me, I've tried the whole growth thing.

I've built a brand, and have my name out there, wherever 'there' is.

I'm on more social media networks that you can poke a stick at, and my email list is growing like it's on steroids.

I've recorded webinars, podcasts and videos.

I've spoken at workshops, and networked my furry little bum off.

I've even built new businesses, created courses, and started selling products.

But the truth is, it's not all unicorns and sunshine.

BEING AN ENTREPRENEUR ISN'T ALL IT'S CRACKED UP TO BE

Those courses I run with six-figure launches? Think about how much content I need to create and update to make them work. Think about the promotion involved in finding new customers, and the work I have to do to support those who've signed up.

Managing those much-loved membership groups is time consuming, particularly when sorting out all the diplomacy issues.

Speaking gigs can be costly (unless you're getting paid the big bucks), nerve wracking, and hugely disruptive to family life. They also play hell with your metabolism and your health.

And don't forget that as well as the three days of intensive 'humaning' (which I find exhausting), there's also the time I have to spend making myself presentable for these events. (Remember those eyebrows down my back?)

And while the podcasts are a lot of fun, they take a huge amount of time and resources to produce. And I'm still not sure what impact (if any) they're having on my business.

Of course, there's nothing like the BoobThrill of PayPalPing while you're not working. You pop your iPhone in your bra so you can listen to a podcast[15], and feel a strange quiver every ten minutes or so when people sign up to or buy your things.

But you're also dealing with imposter syndrome – the crippling moment you realise the collective knowledge of the group you're talking to is far greater than your own.

And I've already mentioned the copycats, the emotional ups and downs, the stress and the haters.

After a while you start to feel like too little butter spread across too much bread.

IT'S IMPORTANT TO BE YOUR OWN TYPE OF ENTREPRENEUR

In the past few years I've realised that I don't want to build a business empire, and I'm not aiming for global domination. I'm quite happy in my cosy little cul-de-sac, and have no desire to be the next 'somebody'. After all, I'm doing pretty damn good so far. What's wrong with being just me – a happy, financially secure nobody?

With six-figure incomes now irrelevant, and everyone aiming for seven-figure launches and eight-figure incomes, I've decided to bow out.

Over the next few months I'll be scaling back my growth, and focusing on consolidation instead.

I'll be:

---

[15] I've since learned this is not good for general boob health.

- Focusing on the business I have instead of looking for new opportunities
- Working on quality, not quantity
- Looking at what I've got instead of thinking about what lies beyond

I don't know where I'll be in five or ten years' time. And as you probably guessed I don't have an exit plan.

But I want to reclaim the bits of my job I love and enjoy. I want to spend less time working on my business and more time working in my business.

Because I don't want a bigger, fatter business. I want a smaller, leaner, more caring one.

WHAT THEY SAY 

If you're not making big moves you're a victim of small thinking. You need to take your competitors' ideas and turn them into your own soaring skyscrapers. You need to build an empire, take over the world, and earn more money.

WHAT I SAY 

I've realised I'll never have enough time or a big enough team to do everything. Even if I did, I no longer have the drive to push that business behemoth forward. (To be honest, I'm not sure I ever did.)

If it comes down to going big or going home I'm happy to go home, make a cup of tea and relax.

CONCLUSION
I'M A PROUD MISFIT ENTREPRENEUR

As you've probably gathered, my idea of a successful entrepreneur isn't someone who jets around the world giving TED talks and works only four hours a week.

I believe how you define success is entirely up to you. You don't need a grand strategy, a carefully polished personal brand, or a morning yoga routine.

My version of entrepreneurism involves frantically typing emails on my phone at the Coles checkout and dry shampooing my greasy fringe seconds before an important video call. But I'm okay with that.

I'm doing the best I can with the time I have. And so far that's been more than good enough.

Writing this book has made me realise that running a business is an adventure. And often the best parts of the adventure are when you become lost, fall down a ravine and get attacked by wolves.

At the risk of tooting my own pipes, I've achieved a fair bit. But it's very rare for me to stop, take stock and pat myself on the back (especially with these tiny T-Rex-like arms of mine).

I started this book thinking I wasn't an entrepreneur at all. But now I realise that I am. A scruffy, disorganised, tired and erratic entrepreneur, but an entrepreneur none the less.

Entrepreneurs come in all shapes, sizes, and shades of teeth whiteness. And what I've learned in my time as a business human is that trying to follow someone else's methodology to the letter isn't a good idea.

Because they are them, and you are you. And while it's fine to pick up some hints and tips, buying into a program to replicate someone else's version of success is likely to be a huge failure.

The other major lesson I've learned is that not all entrepreneurs are created equal. There are many levels of success, and they aren't all measured by the number of zeros on your tax bill.

Being an entrepreneur is about taking risks and trying new things to make money. But it doesn't have to mean launching a multimillion dollar ecourse. It can be something small like taking a risk on a new product, or trying out a FB ad campaign.

The true entrepreneur doesn't give a damn about what the others are doing. They're blazing their own trail, building their own business empire or cul-de-sac, and enjoying the journey rather than fretting about the destination.

I hope this book has made you feel a little more comfortable in your entrepreneurial skin. And if not, then don't call yourself one. Leave that lanyard on the registration table and write your own name badge.

Or just scribble 'Misfit' before 'Entrepreneur' and join my gang.

GLOSSARY

4-HOUR WORK WEEK: The amount of time most parents can work between effing school pick-ups.

A/B TESTING: Testing two things against each other. Like in the Vampire Diaries when you can't decide if you prefer Damon or the other one, so you line them up and compare eyes, and teeth. Talked about a lot when it comes to landing pages and email subject lines.

ALIGN: These days everyone is aligning their business with other businesses. For me this conjures up images of people sidling up to other people at parties and laughing without knowing what everyone is laughing about. It's awkward and weird, so don't use it.

AMAZON BEST-SELLER: You gave away a thousand copies of your book, and then kept refreshing the screen until you hit the top of some obscure category on Amazon long enough to take the obligatory screen shot.

I hope this book becomes an Amazon best-seller in the 'Snarky, bitter business books' category.

AMPLIFY: To turn up the volume on your marketing to an irritatingly loud roar that gives your customers a headache.

AUTHENTIC: To be a true entrepreneur you must be authentic. And then you must authentically tell people how authentic you are on a regular basis.

AUTOMATE: The true entrepreneur flicks a switch at the start of January and doesn't do a god damn thing for the rest of the year because their business is entirely automated. (See also integrate.)

ACTIVATION: The activation phase usually comes after the planning phase, which is after the strategy phase but before the feedback phase. Phased out? Me too.

BIG GIRL PANTS: Apparently we should pull these on before we do anything scary. No thongs allowed, and going commando is definitively a no-no. (Note: There's no such thing as big boy pants.)

BOOTSTRAPPING: Starting a business with no money. In earlier times it was called being poor.

BOSS LADY: I know lots of you love this. And I get that it's kind of cute. But like its vile partner in crime 'Mumpreneur', the fact women have to be 'boss ladies' instead of just 'bosses' irks me. And if you use 'boss lady' and 'sassy' in the same sentence, I'll probably swallow my own tongue in disgust.

BRUSHER (FONT): The paint brush font you see everywhere that should be used on all memes, especially those telling you to dream big. The preferred colour is gold.

COACH: Someone who's read one article about a given subject and now thinks they can charge $150 an hour to teach you about it. Warning: likely to post a lot of motivational memes.

COLLABORATION: No, you can't just work with someone. You have to collaborate or, if you really want to be an entrepreneur, set up a joint venture. You must both be willing to talk endlessly about the collaboration, retweet like a man possessed, and name drop each other every five minutes.

CORE VALUES: The 'solid as oak principles' your business stands for. Your copywriter wrote them for you, and they're on your about page. No one knows what they are, least of all you. You think one of them may be about toast.

DIGITAL NOMAD: Someone who posts images of themselves on tropical beaches with their laptop just to show off and make you feel bad.

DISRUPT: To break away from the commonplace and do something totally out there, crazy and incongruous. Synonyms: irritate, annoy, show off.

ENGAGE: People no longer read your blog posts or like your tweets. They 'engage with your content' instead. Just another wanky marketing buzzword.

FUNNEL: I can't write a definition for this. It just sounds too filthy. (See also Sales funnel.)

GURU: See **Ninja**.

GODDESS: See **Soulful**.

GROWTH HACKING: No, it's not sawing that crusty lump off the bottom of your foot. Instead it's like taking a big bowl of idea spaghetti and hurling it at the wall. You see which ideas stick, and which flop on the floor. It's about trying all the things quickly, and without regret. And then grabbing the bits that work and running with them. Or something.

HACK: Everything is a hack now, and every day I see a post titled something like "10 ingenious arse-wiping hacks" that includes ingenious hacks such as:

- HACK 1: Use two sheets of paper instead of one to avoid getting poo on your hand.
- HACK 2: Sit on the toilet rather than in the sink to ensure your poo goes in the loo.

These are not hacks. At best they're tips, but more often than not they're just stating the bleeding obvious.

HEART-CENTRED: Rather than being driven by their brain ('brain-centred'), 'heart-centred' business types are driven by the red pumping mass, which makes them better people than you and me. They're still trying to sell you a $10,000 mastermind course, but at least they love you while they're doing it.

I personally think I'm 'spleen-centred', or maybe 'Frazzle-centred'. (Don't know what a Frazzle is? Google it!)

HUSTLE: When I see the word 'hustle' I immediately think of fraudsters and swindlers. But these days it's become the byword for anyone who wants to sell with gumption. Another meaning for hustle is 'to push roughly', which is what I'd like to do to anyone who uses this word.

INBOX ZERO: A mythical tale achieved only by people who haven't given anybody their email address.

INNER CIRCLE: Just like the outer circle, only more expensive to join.

INTEGRATE: All your systems should integrate with each other, and synchronise with your social media and email marketing. I'll charge you $10,000 to illustrate this by drawing circles with the words 'email' and 'website' in them, and then drawing wiggly lines leading from each circle.

JOURNEY: See Story.

LEAD MAGNET: A thing that lures people into your 'Funnel'. It could be a webinar, a downloadable thing or a free consult. I really wanted to write something funny for this definition, but it's just too boring.

LIKE LADDER: A popular activity in Mumpreneur groups, which involves posting your Facebook page in a stream of 8,567 other Facebook pages in the hope one sad sucker will 'like' it. Achieves nothing, but you still come back every week and do it again.

MAVEN: No idea. Might be one of the vampires in Twilight.

MASTERMIND: A collection of people who've paid an absurd amount of money to suck success juice from the teat of some sleek entrepreneur type.

MINDSET: Our way of thinking, which we must be keen to change and improve. In the old days people didn't have mindsets. They were too busy trying not to be eaten by dinosaurs.

MOVERS AND SHAKERS: A group of Mumpreneurs at a networking event waiting for the free wine to be given out.

NETWORKING: Standing in a room full of people you don't like and trying to eat a mini quiche with one hand while giving out limp business cards with the other. (Note: May involve drinking too much wine, telling the hot dude from your business Facebook group that you really admire him, and then trying to touch his face.)

NINJA: A ninja (or shinobi) was a covert agent or mercenary in feudal Japan. The functions of the ninja include: espionage, sabotage, infiltration, assassination and guerrilla warfare.

But if you're a marketing ninja or an SEO ninja, you're really just a marketing manager or an SEO consultant. Yes it's boring, but adding 'ninja' to your title doesn't make you sound sharper or quicker than the rest. It just makes you sound like a twat.

Similarly, you should avoid using words such as 'icon', 'rockstar' and 'guru'. (Unless you actually are Jesus, Bono or Maharishi Mahesh Yogi, in which case go for it.)

OPT IN: Similar to 'lead magnet'.

PASSIONATE: A business owner who tries to touch your thigh when you meet them for a briefing.

PASSIVE INCOME: A product that earns you a six-figure income while you sleep. It may take eight months of 40-hour weeks to create, but we don't talk about that bit.

PIVOT: To tweak your business so it goes in a different direction (e.g. "I used to be a dancer on a cruise ship, but I pivoted into being a heart-centred business coach").

SASSY: Quite literally my most hated business word of all time. And those who use it are generally the most tedious people you'll ever meet.

SALES FUNNEL: A greasy tube that becomes progressively narrower, leading your victims from the free thing 'lead magnet' to the gazillion dollar thing 'mastermind'.

SCALE: Something you get in your kettle in areas with hard water.

SIDE HUSTLE: Not an 80s dance move, but rather a side thingy you do to support your main thingy. (See also Hustle.)

SIX FIGURES: Refers to how much moolah you're shoving down your pants every minute of the day. Ideally you should have a six-figure launch, a six-figure ecourse, and be earning seven figures before you have your morning Weetabix.

You don't need to prove that you make six figures. You just need to say it – a lot. You should provide an exact figure (such as $228,981) to make it sound more profitable. But never reveal that only 7% of those six figures is actually profit.

SOLUTIONS: You no longer provide services. You provide solutions. But if you actually use this word you are a problem, not a solution.

SOULFUL: Soulful entrepreneurs generally have more soul than you and less money. Often fond of dreamcatchers, organic muffins and hessian underwear. (See also Heart-centred.)

STORY: (Synonym: journey) I like stories with interesting protagonists who fight dragons, have invisibility cloaks, and ride across clifftops with flowing locks. And so the story of your journey as "A mum who started a wigwam knitting business to have more time to spend with her kids" would be put straight in the bargain bin.

People do connect with stories, but only if they're interesting. And I'm afraid yours doesn't cut the mustard.

And just as you should call a spade a spade, you should call your About page your About page, not 'My Story'.

SYNERGY: I recommend you regularly leverage the synergies you find in business, preferably as frequently as you change your toothbrush.

TRANSFORM: Your business cannot change. Instead it must transform like a fat greasy caterpillar into a glorious entrepreneurial butterfly (with those aggressively white teeth we've already spoken about).

And its variant, Transformational, can be used to express orgasmically awesome stuff (e.g. "This ebook of five copywriting tips that my hamster could have written will be transformational to your business").

TRIBE: I blame Seth Godin for this one. We no longer find customers. Instead we 'attract our tribe' – a group of like-minded people who 'are all individuals' and yet spout the same mantra in the same brushstroke-fonted memes.

I refuse to have a tribe. Instead I have a gang with shiny jackets and flick knives.

TRIPWIRE: A low-cost item you sell to get people on your hallowed list so you can flog them your big expensive thing. Much like having them trip over your door mat and then rifling through their pockets while they're struggling to get up.

UP-LEVEL: To take your business to the next level, as in "Up-level your coaching business with this simple trick".

WEBINAR: A 60-minute presentation with the promise of revealing useful information, but in fact just an opportunity to relentlessly toot your own horn. (Note: It's vital to send 27 reminder emails before the webinar starts, and 23 guilt-inducing 'you missed it/you left early' emails afterwards).

Note: Extra points for technology fails, and pre-recorded webinars pretending to be live.

> *Presenter: "Hello. We have 500 people on the webinar. Say hello, and where you're from."*

> *Sole audience member: "Hello, I'm Alan from Sydney."*

> *Presenter: "Hi, Sue. Hello, Janine. Welcome Kevin. I can see Canada, London, Paris. How's the weather in Berlin, Rudolph?"*

Group chat: *<Silence>*

Presenter: *"The comments are coming in so fast. <Laughs for no reason.> Okay, let's get started. I'm going to start by telling you my story..."*

Remember, it's essential to waste as much of your watcher's time as possible. So it's a good idea to repeatedly promise 'some big thing' at the end. Ideally you should mention it every two or three seconds. And then fail to deliver it.

WITH THANKS TO

Of course, I wanted to take this final page to thank the people who have made this book possible:

My **mum and dad**, for being my first readers and for always being so supportive in everything I do.

Kelly Exeter: www.kellyexeter.com. My wonderful structural editor, who pushed me to finish the first draft by threatening to donate to Donald Trump if I didn't.

Bill Harper: www.sharpercopy.com. My fastidious editor, who took my messy scribbles and turned them into polished prose.

Kate Buckland: www.oneandonecreative.com.au. Designer extraordinaire, who puts up with my 'Make it pop' and 'Can the logo be bigger?' comments and creates such beautiful work.

Sharon Chisholm: www.yourmindhealthmatters.com. My Misfit Entrepreneur Community buddy, who's makes me laugh and snort pretty much every day.

Robert Gerrish: www.flyingsolo.com.au My trusty advisor all these years. Thank you so much for agreeing to write my foreword, Robert.

Marco Gatta: www.techniqueinteractive.com.au My trusty developer and business buddy who I think I speak to more each week than I do my husband.

My early readers

- Melinda Samson | www.clickwinningcontent.com.au
- Loren Bartley | www.impactiv8.com.au and www.businessaddicts.com
- Maria Doyle | www.mariadoyle.com
- Kerry Pietrobon | www.Harlowstore.com
- Natasha Vanzetti | www.natashavanzetti.com
- Yael Keon | www.mixsavvymarketing.com
- Carly Findlay | www.carlyfindlay.com
- Dani Tamati | www.therh.com.au
- Eva Schafroth | www.evaschafroth.com
- Kate Merryweather | www.dotcomwords.com.au
- Lucy Davies | www.websitesbylucy.co.uk
- Dawn Kofie | www.zestywriting.com
- Kylie Saunder | www.kyliesaunder.com
- Katie Wyatt | www.katiewyatt.me

My wonderful handsome, kind, funny husband, who is the ultimate misfit entrepreneur. Thank you for inspiring me to give up the day job in the first place, and for just being the amazing human you are.

My son. I wouldn't have ever taken the plunge into running my own business if you hadn't appeared in my womb. Thanks for the cuddles and the giggles, and for helping me to remember what's important in life, like Pokemon, Dot-to-Dots and splashing in the pool.

Oh, and just another quick mention for **Pamplemousse**, because dog, cute, furry.